SLIC SOLUTIONS™ FOR CONFLICT

SLIC SOLUTIONS™ FOR CONFLICT

SETTING LIMITS & IMPOSING CONSEQUENCES IN 2½ STEPS

BILL EDDY, LCSW, ESQ.
Ekaterina RICCI, MDR, MLS

an imprint of High Conflict Institute Press
Scottsdale, Arizona

Testimonials

SLIC Solutions distills conflict mastery into a simple, repeatable 2½-step system—set the limit, impose the consequence, and add empathy when it helps—brought to life with scenarios from family rooms to boardrooms. As a true-crime producer-showrunner who's dealt with high-conflict personalities on and off camera, I recognize how practical and protective this playbook is. It teaches you to hold the line—calmly, clearly, and firmly—without becoming the villain in the story. A must-have for anyone who needs to set boundaries with grace.

—**CHRISTOPHER GIDEZ,** True Crime Producer-Showrunner & Content Marketing Editor–Director

As a CEO advisor, I've seen how workplace conflicts can quietly erode productivity and morale—but this book changes that. Its clear, actionable framework and 2½-step method make it easy to manage high-conflict behavior with both confidence and respect. The real-world examples ring true, offering practical tools to resolve disputes while strengthening team culture. Every leader who values clarity, accountability, and impact should read this. Applied early, it can even help prevent client escalations and costly legal disputes.

—**ALI PARNIAN,** Founder & CEO, Impact Delivered

Dealing with difficult people can feel like playing chess for the first time. Beginners are mostly reactive and have no fundamental strategy for the game. Bill Eddy and Ekaterina Ricci have given those of us struggling with high conflict people a straightforward structure that enables us to stop reacting, set limits, and begin engaging effectively and strategically, while also providing realistic examples of applications in a broad cross section of human interactions.

—**SIMONE F. HABERSTOCK,** J.D., CPA, Mediator, 2024 Ellen Cowell Leadership Award Winner

Bill Eddy's approach to conflict has been transformative for us. Set boundaries, analyze the consequences, and use EAR Statements when appropriate. We found his guidance leads to outcomes that are both healthy and safe. The book offers a clear, concise, and doable set of guidelines—and it works! The examples are realistic and reflect common situations faced by everyone. The solutions are practical and easy to apply. You don't need a Ph.D. in psychology to implement Bill's suggestions. This book should be required reading for anyone dealing with conflictual situations.

—**MARK GLICK,** Professor of Economics, University of Utah, and **ALBA CRUZ,** Teacher

Having worked alongside Bill Eddy for many years, I have witnessed firsthand his rare ability to translate complex conflict dynamics into practical, actionable tools. Together with Ekaterina Ricci, he now offers *SLIC Solutions for Conflict*—a method that empowers professionals to set boundaries and enforce consequences with both clarity and respect. This book not only completes *The CARS Method*® but also directly addresses the urgent need for effective strategies to manage high-conflict behavior across professions. It is an indispensable guide for anyone committed to constructive resolution.

—**MICHAEL LOMAX,** JD, International Speaker & Trainer, and Co-Author of *Mediating High Conflict Disputes*

Publisher's Note

This publication is designed to provide accurate and authoritative information about the subject matters covered. It is sold with the understanding that neither the authors nor publisher are rendering legal, mental health or other professional services, either directly or indirectly. If expert assistance, legal services or counseling is needed, the services of a competent professional should be sought. Neither the authors nor the publisher shall be liable or responsible for any loss or damage allegedly arising as a consequence of your use or application of any information or suggestions in this book.

Printed in the United States of America
First Edition

Cover design by Julian León, The Missive
Interior Design by Jeffrey Fuller, Shelfish

ISBN (print): 9781950057474
ISBN (ebook): 9781950057498
Library of Congress Control Number: 2025945393

Unhooked Media, 7701 E. Indian School Rd., Ste. F, Scottsdale, AZ 85251
www.unhookedmedia.com

Also by Bill Eddy

Conflict Communication Series:

BIFF: Quick Responses to High Conflict People, Their Personal Attacks and Social Media Meltdowns

BIFF for Co-Parent Communication

BIFF for Lawyers

BIFF at Work

Calming Upset People with EAR

Mediating High Conflict Disputes

High Conflict People in Legal Disputes

Managing High Conflict People in Court

The Future of Family Court

It's All Your Fault at Work! Managing Narcissists and other High-Conflict People

5 Types of People Who Can Ruin Your Life

Why We Elect Narcissists & Sociopaths—and How We Can Stop

Dating Radar

So, What's Your Proposal

It's All Your Fault! 12 Tips for Managing People Who Blame Others for Everything

Don't Alienate the Kids! Raising Resilient Children While Avoiding High Conflict Divorce

Splitting: Protecting Yourself While Divorcing Someone with Borderline or Narcissistic Personality Disorder

Splitting America

New Ways for Families in Separation and Divorce:
Professional Guidebook
Parent Workbook
Collaborative Parent Workbook
Decision Skills Class Instructor's Manual & Workbook
Pre-Mediation Coaching Manual & Workbook
Online Course Coaching Manual

New Ways for Work Coaching Manual & Workbook

New Ways for Life Instructor Guide & Youth Journal

To my wife Alice, and to my many clients who showed me the pain and frustration of dealing with high-conflict people in their lives and who showed me that they could successfully learn to protect themselves and grow by setting limits and imposing consequences.

—Bill

To my dad, Victor, who never stopped believing in me; to my sister, Yulia, who never stopped supporting me; and to my mom, Anna, who never stopped encouraging me to reach higher.

—Ekaterina

Contents

INTRODUCTION

This is the fourth book in a series of simple techniques for managing high-conflict situations, developed by the High Conflict Institute, a training institute for professionals and anyone dealing with a conflict. The Institute's trainings include four simple techniques that help implement the *CARS Method*® of conflict resolution. Here is a brief introduction to the *CARS Method*, the four simple techniques, and the authors of this book.

The *CARS Method*® and Four Simple Techniques

The *CARS Method* stands for ***Connecting*** with another person to calm the conflict, ***Analyzing*** options to manage or resolve the conflict, ***Responding*** to hostility or misinformation that is often present, and ***Setting*** limits on negative behavior and imposing consequences when necessary. These four general approaches can be used separately, some together, or all of them depending on the conflict situation, in no particular order. Very briefly, here are the four techniques and related books:

EAR Statements (Connecting)

A simple technique for connecting with an upset person or others in a conflict is a statement that shows empathy, attention, and/or respect *(an EAR Statement™)*. Such a statement can calm them down enough so that you can focus on finding solutions to a conflict. You can use these when someone is angry at someone else or is angry at you. The High Conflict Institute instruction book on this technique is: *Calming Upset People with EAR: How Statements Showing Empathy, Attention and Respect Can Quickly Defuse a Conflict* (Unhooked Books, 2021), which includes 28 sample conversations.

Making Proposals in Three Steps (Analyzing)

In a high-conflict situation or any conflict, it helps to get away from emotions and focus on options for what to do to resolve the conflict. Analyzing choices or generating options can help. Also, asking an upset or difficult person to make a proposal often helps them focus on finding a solution. The instruction book on our 3-step technique for making proposals and decisions is: *So, What's Your Proposal? Shifting High-Conflict People from Blaming to Problem-Solving in 30 Seconds* (Unhooked Books, 2014), which includes over a dozen examples of making proposals.

BIFF Response® (Responding)

Whether someone is writing a hostile email or simply expressing some misinformation to you, a *BIFF Response®* can help. These are usually in writing and are *Brief, Informative, Friendly, and Firm.* There are several instruction books on this technique in different settings: The first, general book for everyone is *BIFF: Quick Responses to High-Conflict People, Their Personal Attacks, Hostile Email and Social Media Meltdowns* (Unhooked Books, 2011, 2014). The three other *BIFF* books focus on divorced parents *(BIFF for CoParent Communication)*, the workplace *(BIFF at Work)*, and legal professionals *(BIFF for Lawyers and Law Offices)*. Each of these books contains about 30 examples. Look for more books on this technique over the next few years.

SLIC Solutions™ (Setting Limits)

SLIC Solutions is the fourth technique in the series and is often the most important one. Some people can't stop themselves from offensive or harmful behavior, so others need to stop them. This technique can be used with anyone in your life and can be learned at almost any age. You are about to read our book on this subject: *SLIC Solutions to Conflict: Setting Limits and Imposing Consequences in 2½ Steps* (Unhooked Books, 2025). This book contains numerous examples of setting limits and imposing consequences.

Who Are We?

Bill is a therapist, lawyer, mediator, and the Director of Innovation for the High Conflict Institute, a private company he co-founded in 2008 with Megan Hunter, MBA. He was a therapist for twelve years (Licensed Clinical Social Worker), then became a lawyer (Certified Family Law Specialist for 15 years), then became the Senior Family Mediator at the National Conflict Resolution Center based in San Diego, California for 15 years. He is the developer of the *CARS Method* and the specific techniques described in these four books.

He is also the developer of several other methods: *New Ways for Families®*, *New Ways for Mediation™*, *New Ways for Work®* (with L. Georgi DiStefano, LCSW), and *New Ways for Life™* (with Susie Rayner, FDR). In each of these methods, "New Ways" means new skills to help manage *one's own* behavior, in contrast to the CARS Method which is designed to help manage *other people's* behavior. Bill is also the author or co-author of twenty books and manuals dealing with high-conflict behavior and situations. He loves to teach and has provided trainings to lawyers, judges, mediators, therapists, and others in forty states and over a dozen countries, and consultations to over a thousand individuals.

Ekaterina has a background in microbiology, immunology, and molecular genetics. She has spent years studying how bacteria and human cells interact—with each other, their hosts, and within complex environments. This scientific foundation shapes her current focus on how biology influences human conflict. Ekaterina is particularly fascinated by how internal factors such as diet, inflammation, and the gut-brain connection affect emotional regulation, impulsivity, and perception—often without our awareness. While she fully recognizes the central role of psychological, environmental, and socio-political factors in conflict, she believes biology is an often-overlooked layer that helps explain why some individuals are more reactive or dysregulated than others in a conflict. Ekaterina was a student in Bill's law school course on Psychology of Conflict Communication at Pepperdine University's Straus Institute of Dispute Resolution. She did an internship with the High Conflict Institute and then joined the team.

This Book

This book grew out of a discussion Bill and Ekaterina had at a conference dinner in 2024. Bill's book *Our New World of Adult Bullies: How to Spot Them – How to Stop Them*, had just come out and Ekaterina suggested that there should be a workbook to go along with it. She believed that people would need lots of practice to face bullies and set limits on them. Because of her interest in combining biology with conflict resolution, we got into a good discussion of how the brain learns and the need to repeatedly *practice* when learning new skills—especially in conflict situations when our brains want to shut down. Soon after, we started writing this book.

Together we have prepared a wide range of everyday situations for you for practicing the *SLIC Solutions* technique. Some examples are totally made up, some are based on real life, and some are taken directly from real events. Feel free to read the book through from start to finish, by the end of which you will have memorized the technique. Or jump ahead to the section that most applies to you. This book only makes suggestions, as you are responsible for fitting these general principles to your own conflict situation. Just keep the fundamental idea in mind that setting limits on its own doesn't always work. Instead, think ahead to the consequences you would impose if the other person ignores your limit-setting and how you will present it and implement it, if necessary.

We wish you all the best!

—Bill Eddy
—Ekaterina Ricci

CHAPTER 1

PREPARING TO ASSERT YOURSELF

Have you ever had a conversation like this:

YOU: *Please stop talking to me that way. You're bothering me.*
THEM: *No, I'll talk to you any way I want!*

Or this:

YOU: *You know there's a rule (or law) against doing that. You shouldn't do that.*
THEM: *Don't be so fussy. No one is going to know and no one is going to stop me.*

Or this:

YOU: *Hey! Leave her alone! You're being rude and inconsiderate!*
THEM: *Mind your own business. I'll treat her however I please.*

The world has changed. The rules have changed. And many people ignore the limits that have been set on them—in families, at work, in communities, and anywhere. That's why we wrote this book. Some people ignore the rules and don't pay attention to the limits that others set on their behavior (we think of them as *high-conflict people or HCPs)* ***unless*** a meaningful consequence will follow if they violate the limit. For this reason, we developed the simple technique we call *SLIC Solutions™ for Conflict: Setting Limits and Imposing Consequences in 2½ steps.* Let's look at some typical situations where this method might be useful.

Everyday Life Dilemmas

Pam doesn't know what to do. A co-worker with more seniority makes her dread going in each day. Kathleen criticizes the smallest thing Pam does, uses an arrogant tone of voice, and publicly blames Pam for Kathleen's own mistakes. Should Pam try to set limits on Kathleen's behavior? What kind of consequences could she impose? Will they even work? Or should she try to avoid Kathleen as much as possible and just suck it up when she can't? Or should she just quit?

Reggie's teenage daughter is starting to talk back to him and bad-mouth him to her siblings. He grew up in a home that was too strict, so he wants to be a more flexible dad, but even he has limits. He wants to set limits on her offensive behavior, but he doesn't know if *she* is really being inappropriate for a modern adolescent or if *he* is being out of line in today's world. He doesn't want to push her away like he feels his parents did with him.

Gerald's wife is increasingly relying on pills from different doctors to get through the day, even though her work doesn't seem stressful to him. She staggers around the house and falls asleep at embarrassing times. She blames him for being away so much and unsupportive when he's at home. When he confronts her about it, she tells him he's part of the problem and that she needs meds to help her cope. He's not sure what to do. He wants her to stop depending on the medications and stop blaming him. He also doesn't want anyone else to know about this problem.

Jennifer's ex-husband owes her a $10,000 equalizing payment from their divorce settlement agreement. It's been two years since he was supposed to pay it and she still hasn't seen any of it. He keeps saying he'll get around to it, but he doesn't take any action to make it happen. He has a higher income and can afford it, but he just won't. Should she go to court? Or will that just make him angrier and more resistant? Will the court even enforce its own orders?

Pam, Reggie, Gerald, and Jennifer are four of the thirty examples in this book of people facing situations in which setting limits and imposing consequences would be appropriate. But which limits and what consequences? And how do they get up the nerve to follow through? This book will help with all of this.

The Problem

On the one hand, more people than ever before can do almost anything in today's world as an individual. Overall, this is a good thing. There is more individual freedom, flexibility, travel, health, opportunities, and creativity. But on the other hand, there is less social responsibility and some people have become much more aggressive toward others. Many people overstep and violate other people's rights and boundaries. This can actually limit some people's choices, health, and opportunities. Maybe you have experienced this yourself already.

In the not-too-distant past, most people in the family, community, and nation knew and followed and enforced the same basic rules throughout their lives, from the youngest child (*You're not allowed to do that!*) to the oldest citizen (*It's always been done this way!*). But as standards have changed and enforcement has weakened, it's time for everyone to learn some new skills so we can rely more on ourselves for our own protection and growth.

That's the bad news, but also the good news because these skills don't have to be hard to learn.

The Solution

The solution is learning and practicing skills of *Setting Limits and Imposing Consequences in 2½ Steps*. And you can do it! Rather than just responsibly managing your own behavior, this book will teach you how to possibly manage or at least influence the behavior of those around you who are violating your rules and boundaries or simply ignoring the rules that do exist that are no longer being enforced by others. This book will teach you how to do all of this and increase your confidence at the same time.

In order to keep it simple, especially in stressful situations, the technique we have developed—*SLIC Solutions*—is easy to remember. We have narrowed it down to just 2½ steps to think of when you are dealing with a difficult situation:

SLIC Solutions™

Step 1: **S**etting the **L**imit
(while mentioning the consequences);

Step 2: **I**mposing the **C**onsequences; and

Step 2½: **EAR Statement** (or Not – about half the time).

Of course, simple doesn't necessarily mean easy. This technique takes practice and being creative, so we will break it down into parts in the next three chapters. We give you details on how to generally apply each step, then the rest of the chapters give 30 examples of using *SLIC Solutions* in various settings of daily life. But first we want to give you some background knowledge and help you build your strength and confidence for setting limits and imposing consequences. This can be frightening in many situations, but with practice it gets easier.

Dealing with High-Conflict Behavior

In the last few years, there has been an increase in the number of people with *high-conflict behavior* around the world who cannot stop themselves. Now all of us need to learn how to stop them or redirect them, individually and with the help of others. Here is the common pattern of high-conflict behavior:

1. ***A preoccupation with blaming others.***
   (While taking no responsibility themselves.)
2. ***A lot of all-or-nothing thinking.***
   (In terms of problems and solutions.)
3. ***Unmanaged or intense emotions.***
   (Whether obvious or not, these often drive their behavior way out of bounds.)
4. ***Extreme behaviors.***
   (This may include things that 90% of people would never do.)

When this becomes a repeated pattern of behavior it means that it may be embedded in their personality. In this case, we think of them as having a *high-conflict personality* or being a *high-conflict person* (HCP). This means it helps to narrow your approach to dealing with them. We estimate that approximately 10% of people are potential HCPs. Their personalities play a big role in pushing other people's limits and boundaries in today's world. HCPs will be some of the most difficult people for you when setting your limits and imposing your consequences. Yet using the simple *SLIC Solutions* method may help you do just that.

We're telling you about HCPs, not to be judgmental but to help you avoid being surprised by their sometimes-shocking behavior, to avoid over-reacting, and to give a reasonable response. They may be good, smart people, but they have difficulty with conflicts and tend to escalate or prolong them unnecessarily. In a sense, they have a different operating system when it comes to conflicts with others.

HCPs always have *targets of blame* to whom they direct their challenging behavior. Their targets are usually people in close relationships with them (like spouses, parents, children, dating partners, close co-workers, close neighbors) or people in positions of authority (police, government agencies, heads of organizations).

Bullies

Bullies are the *most* high-conflict people. They have the four conflict behaviors above, *plus* a drive to dominate or destroy others in their lives. They can be especially aggressive in trying to get you to do things you don't want to do—in which case you will want to set limits and need to impose consequences in order to stop or redirect them. Everything in this book about high-conflict people and behavior applies especially to bullies. (For more on understanding and managing bullies, see Bill's book *Our New World of Adult Bullies: How to Spot Them – How to Stop Them*).

However, you can try SLIC Solutions with almost anyone, regardless of their personality and conflict behavior.

What to Avoid

If you suspect that you are dealing with someone with a high-conflict personality, there are four things to try to avoid in narrowing your approach. However, you can avoid these with anyone so you never need to determine if someone is a high-conflict person. We call these the Four Fuhgeddaboudits.

Avoid These Four Fuhgeddaboudits

1. ***Trying to give them insight into their own behavior.*** *(This triggers extreme defensiveness. Instead, focus outward on what to do.)*

2. ***Focusing on emotions.***
   (This puts them in touch with many unresolved and angry feelings and shuts down logical thinking. Instead, steer away from emotions and focus on new behavior.)

3. ***Focusing on the past.***
   (They easily get stuck in the past, arguing and complaining about everyone else. Instead, focus on future behavior and what to do now.)

4. ***Labelling them anything.***
   (Don't tell them that you think they are a high-conflict person, a bully, or anything else. This can trigger intense defensiveness, rather than self-reflection. Instead, focus on what to do going forward. Focus on setting limits and imposing consequences.)

An Assertive Approach

By avoiding these Four Fuhgeddaboudits, it will be easier to stay narrowly focused on simply setting limits on others and imposing consequences if they violate them. We're not used to trying to manage others' behavior and most people don't want others to try to manage theirs. So, it's easy to get distracted and fall into having an argument instead. With this in mind, it's important to recognize the difference between assertive and aggressive approaches.

An *aggressive approach* is used by people who want to dominate or destroy another person or their reputation. You don't need to do that in order to set limits, even if you want to do that. If you ask "When can I punch him in the nose?" the answer is: Never! It's certainly tempting and understandable that you want to respond to someone's aggressive behavior with your own aggressive behavior, but that often can boomerang on you. If you are aggressive back, it looks like *you* are being the aggressive person even though you are just responding.

High-conflict people are especially good at pointing fingers at others, when they in fact started the conflict. Don't give them ammunition to use against you.

An *assertive approach* is the preferred approach: emotionally calm, but firm, by simply stating what the limit is that you are setting. For example: "You can't speak to me using those words or that tone of voice." Same for imposing the consequence: "If you don't stop, I will have to end this conversation." If you have to, you can raise your voice enough to be heard, but don't act or look outraged or out of control. Instead, you want to look totally in control, clear, and confident about what you mean. When you are dealing with a high-conflict person, they often get energized by your frustration and upset emotions, sensing that they have successfully manipulated you into an angry but helpless response. Helpless anger rewards them and energizes their emotions. Of course, no one is perfect at this, so just try to do the best you can to *be* in control and *look* in control of yourself.

A *passive approach* is the third way that people often act in difficult situations. This usually means no response or showing a helpless, frightened, or immobilized response. This is very common and a built-in survival mechanism. However, try to overcome this as soon as possible, because this especially feeds high-conflict people as they feel they can now dominate you and manipulate you. Instead, if you are being confronted with high-conflict behavior and don't know yet how you want to respond, you can just calmly say: "I'll get back to you on this" or "I'll talk with you later." Then figure out afterward how you want to respond or talk to someone to get some ideas. In some safe situations, you might laugh or shake your head or just walk away. This way you are signaling that you are not going to passively accept this and are not shaken by what was said or done, even though you may not have said a word.

Setting Limits AND Imposing Consequences

An essential theme of this book is that setting limits is often not enough, especially if you are dealing with an HCP. They may simply ignore your limit-setting. Therefore, in many cases you will need to let the person know what the *consequence is* if they violate your limit. Then, if they still violate your limit, you will need to impose your consequence.

For example:

Bill was the lawyer for a divorce client who was a victim of domestic violence by her husband. At first her husband did not have a divorce lawyer and there was a restraining order against him having direct contact with his wife. This meant that he would call Bill to negotiate the terms of the divorce, including parenting time with their two children.

When the husband started cursing about his wife when he was talking to Bill, Bill said "You can't talk about my client that way." But the husband kept talking that way, so Bill said "You can't talk about my client that way OR I'll have to end the phone call. It's up to you." (Setting the limit AND informing him about the consequence that would be imposed.) He kept talking that way, so Bill said "You have chosen to end the phone call. Call me when you're ready to talk civilly about my client. Goodbye!" And hung up.

The next day the husband called Bill and started talking about a problem and complained about his wife in the same offensive terms as the day before. Bill said "Remember, if you keep talking about my client that way, I will end the call again." The husband said "No, no. Don't hang up. We really need to solve this problem. I'll try not to say those words." And the husband changed his behavior a little bit to be more respectful.

It took setting the limit (you can't talk that way) AND imposing the consequence (ending the phone call) for the husband to accept the limit. Keep that in mind as you deal with potentially difficult people. Sometimes simply stating the limit is sufficient, but often the consequence is necessary too. Many people don't realize or expect that. Now you know so you can prepare yourself.

Encouraging Statements

Now that we have focused your attention on using an assertive approach to setting your limits and imposing your consequences, let's talk about how to strengthen yourself to do this with confidence. It can always help to get encouraging words from others who like you and agree with your need to set limits on another person's extreme behavior. When that's possible, go for it!

However, this may not always be an option. Sometimes there is no one around or available to give you encouraging words at your time of need. In that case, keep in mind that you can *give yourself* encouraging words—an encouraging statement! Here's a few examples:

"*I NEED to do this, for my own well-being!*"

"*The way I have been treated is unacceptable!
I need to Set Limits!*"

"*No one deserves to be bullied even if they made a mistake.*"

"*I'm a good parent/employee/neighbor/citizen!*"

"*I deserve to be treated with respect.*"

Repeating these out loud to yourself can be very powerful, because the way our brains work is that repetition gets absorbed and becomes more automatic. Putting a Post-it sticker with a short phrase like this on your bathroom mirror can help remind you of your power.

Also, keep in mind that you can give yourself your encouraging statement(s) *while* you are in the middle of setting limits and imposing consequences on the other person. It makes their negative remarks surprisingly less powerful in your brain and makes your statement more powerful in your brain. Try it sometime!

Safety Check

Sometimes, it isn't safe to try to set limits and impose consequences. In such a situation, just get out or at least just silently tell yourself an encouraging statement (such as: "I don't deserve this, but I'm not going to risk confronting this person right now"). Sometimes this is the best choice and you can respect yourself for making a wise decision. Nothing we are saying in this book requires you to attempt to set limits and impose consequences in every situation. "Choose your battles" is often a good phrase to remember as one of your encouraging statements. Safety first.

Practice

The key to effectively setting limits and imposing consequences is practice. The more that you can do this in a matter-of-fact way, the easier it will become part of your routine way of relating to others. While you can practice your general encouraging statement on a regular basis, we suggest that you also prepare for specific situations by practicing with someone supportive before the real conversation in a "role-play" conversation.

For example, you might be preparing to say:

*YOU: "No, I am not going to the store with you, Jenny.
You need to do this on your own."*

Find a friend, family member, consultant, or coach to practice with you. Tell them what you expect Jenny to say when you are setting limits on her, then practice your response with the other person playing Jenny.

*You: "No, I am not going to the store with you, Jenny.
You need to do this on your own."*

Person playing Jenny: "But you have to come with me. You have to change your plans. I can't make this decision without you."

You: As I said, I'm not going to the store with you, Jenny."

Person playing Jenny: "You really don't care do you!"

You: As I said, I'm not going."

Person playing Jenny: "Oh, okay. I get it!"

As demonstrated in this example, after a few back-and-forth statements, the person playing Jenny eventually accepted your limit ("Oh, okay. I get it."). This practice helps you gain confidence that it is appropriate for you to set such a limit. Then, when you are in the real situation and the difficult person persists in resisting your limit setting, you will know that it is okay for you to persist in setting it—and saying less and less each time. As your brain gets more comfortable giving yourself encouraging statements and practicing saying these limit-setting words, you will gain confidence. There will be more on this in Chapter 2.

Conclusion

In today's world, every individual needs to develop and practice skills of *setting limits AND imposing consequences* to protect yourself and to thrive. This can become easier and more routine with practice. There is more high-conflict behavior in the world now because the institutions that used to set limits and impose consequences have weakened (families, communities, national standards) and high-conflict individuals are less restrained than in the past. While this puts a responsibility on everyone to be more assertive about setting their own limits, it also puts a responsibility on all of us to support each other in imposing consequences that fit the situation. You're not alone and these skills are not hard to learn. The rest of this book will teach you how to apply these skills with confidence in numerous everyday life situations.

The examples will give you an opportunity to see what others have done in their unique situations, but also ask yourself what you might do in similar circumstances. There is usually no one right answer, as you need to fit your responses to: who the other person is, what the situation is, and who you are. The SLIC Solutions formula is designed to help in all situations.

CHAPTER 2

STEP 1: SETTING LIMITS

Pam thought about what she could say to Kathleen at work. She really did not appreciate Kathleen's frequent criticisms, especially since Kathleen was not her supervisor but simply another worker with more seniority—she had been there longer. So, Pam spoke with a friend about it and decided on what she would say. She practiced with her friend pretending to be Kathleen and felt more confident after their "role-play" conversation. Then she was ready to respond to Kathleen the next time she wanted to give her unwelcome advice.

> *Kathleen: "You know, Pam, you're doing it wrong. You should do it this way."*
>
> *Pam: "Actually, Kathleen. If you want to give me suggestions then ask me first if I want them. If I say Yes, then go ahead. But if I say No, then it's not a good time. That's what I need. And right now, it's not a good time. I need to be somewhere else, thank you."*
>
> Then Pam walked away. Kathleen was speechless.

Speaking Up

Most of us, most of the time, set limits on ourselves so that we can get along in the world. We stay in our lane. We hold our tongue. We use our inside voice when we're indoors. This is often called self-restraint, self-regulation, or self-discipline. It helps people succeed and get along.

Of course, there are exceptional moments. But when most people accidentally offend us or step on our toes, they usually stop themselves. Sometimes they apologize. Other times we need to speak up and ask if they meant to offend us or made a mistake. Usually this is sufficient with ordinary people. But some people lack these skills of self-restraint and have a *pattern* of stepping on other people's toes or worse on a regular basis, which often causes increasing conflict. Such high-conflict people (HCPs) are in need of external limits and consequences. Therefore, the people around them have to set limits on them for their own protection and to thrive. The focus of this chapter will be on how to set limits on HCPs. But you can use these principles with anyone.

Don't Argue About It

Many people believe that they can simply persuade others to behave differently or to stop their offensive behavior. You might be able to do this with ordinary, reasonable people. However, with HCPs, they typically become defensive or enraged when others set limits on them. In some cases, they are truly oblivious to the impact that they have on others. In many cases they are self-absorbed because they lack empathy, remorse, or self-control, so they see the needs of others as low priority or non-existent.

Therefore, if you set limits on them *they* may feel offended and will argue with you about them. They may try to turn the tables and tell you how offensive *you are*—to make you defensive or to simply distract you. As a reasonable person, you will likely feel surprised and question yourself: "*Am I being too sensitive here? Am I overstepping my bounds in this situation?*" Many reasonable people back off when this happens and go into a period of self-reflection—instead of sticking with appropriate limit setting.

In addition, HCPs are usually preoccupied with past grievances and will bring up as much of the past as they can with a lot of emotional intensity during any conflict. You will need to be prepared for this. HCPs are usually not going to change, especially in response to your feedback. Otherwise, they wouldn't repeatedly increase conflicts and instead would try to resolve them. If they have a high-conflict pattern of behavior, it will increase—not decrease—when you try to set limits on that behavior.

In Pam's example above, she was prepared for Kathleen to object to her limit-setting. Instead of leaving room for an argument, she explained her limit in matter-of-fact terms (ask me before giving me suggestions) and then walked away. She avoided the argument and there really was nothing else that needed to be discussed.

Was she disrespectful because she didn't give Kathleen a chance to respond? No. Pam was under no obligation to listen to Kathleen, who was volunteering her criticism or advice without being asked for it. There was nothing they had to do together at that time, so Pam was free to say her piece and move away. Just confidently walking away was part of what she practiced with her friend, so that she would not hesitate. After that exchange, Kathleen kept her distance for a few days and Pam felt more and more confident that she had done the right thing.

Keep it Simple

You may want to set your own limit on how someone treats you. That's fine. Usually, you can set any limits you want on how others treat you, even if it is different from how others want to be treated. There's a lot of personal choice today. Of course, it helps to check with others to see if you are being reasonable in your limit-setting ideas. That is what Pam did with her friend before confronting Kathleen.

There are organizational limits that apply to everyone. There are other people's limits which may be different from yours or in addition to the organization's. Some limits are complex, like a no-harassment policy. Some people are very uncomfortable in-person and prefer to be communicated with in writing.

In Pam's case above, she kept it simple. She didn't criticize Kathleen, she didn't blame her, and she didn't use a hostile tone. She kept it matter-of-fact with a clear limit: "Ask me first if I want to hear your suggestions." Pam didn't say "You always do this." Avoid *always* and *never* if you want to keep it simple.

Pam also didn't say "You are being rude and inconsiderate." She avoided "you" statements and emphasized "I" statements, like "That's what I need." It's hard to argue with what someone says they need. It's easy to argue with "you" statements that accuse the other person of acting badly, like: "You should know better." That's an admonishment, which doesn't work well when setting limits. The other person will likely respond by saying: "No, YOU should know better."

Setting Limits Without Mentioning Consequences

In Pam's situation, she just set her limit and never mentioned any consequences. If Kathleen accepts her limit, then that was sufficient. If she starts to criticize Pam in the future, Pam can simply say: "Remember, what I told you. Please ask me first if I want a suggestion." In other words, she can repeat and reinforce her limit without having to discuss any consequences.

However, some people do not follow the limit you have set for them. High-conflict people especially ignore the limits others set on them. Then, you have a dilemma. If you tolerate them ignoring your limit, it often emboldens them to violate your limits even more so and treat you more disrespectfully in other areas as well. Therefore, you need to be prepared to impose a consequence if they violate your limits and you may need to point this out to them when you set your limit.

Setting Limits AND Mentioning Consequences

Reggie plans to set a limit on his teenage daughter's disrespectful language with him. He realizes that simply telling her how she should speak to him and about him will have little impact—unless there is a consequence for violating that limit. Tisha is just 14, but after checking with some other parents he concluded that she should still be expected to treat him with respect. Now is the best time for her to learn this lesson rather than hoping she will grow out of it. Of course, her personality won't be completely formed until her 20s, so she doesn't have a high-conflict personality yet, but he doesn't want her to develop one.

> *Tisha: "You know, you're an idiot, Dad! You don't know a thing about what's going on these days."*
>
> *Reggie: "You know, Tisha. You can't talk to me that way anymore. You're growing up and even I have limits."*
>
> *Tisha: "Well, I don't care. You're just f-ing stupid about what's going on in my world. Everybody knows you're the most uncool dad around."*
>
> *Reggie: "Well, if you keep talking to me or about me to your younger brother and sister with those bad words, I'm not going to pay for that trip you want to go on with your class."*
>
> *Tisha: "What the..." She caught herself before she said what he knew she was going to say. "That's not fair!"*
>
> *Reggie: "Let me know if you have any questions about this."*
>
> *Tisha: "NO! I don't have any questions!" And she picked up her cell phone and buried herself in it.*

In this case, the *credible threat* of the consequence of not going on her school trip got her attention. Setting the limit ("You can't talk to me that way") on its own did not work. She escalated from an insult to a curse word. He had thought about what his consequence would be and had it ready when she pushed back. It worked.

Anticipate Push-Back

Try to anticipate push-back and how you will deal with it when you are in a situation in which you need to set limits. You probably know what push-back to expect from familiar people in your life, so that you can prepare and practice what you will say if necessary. There will also be situations with people you don't know where limit setting may be necessary. By thinking ahead and practicing what you will say, you are less likely to be caught by surprise.

It's Okay to Interrupt

When a high-conflict person is behaving badly, it's okay to interrupt their bad behavior. Many (most) people are uncomfortable interrupting someone else from what they are saying or doing. But when they are being inappropriate or harmful, they should be interrupted from doing that. Of course, as explained before, you need to choose your battles and be prepared for push-back. Anticipate that they will not like being interrupted, but be firm in what you have decided to say and do when you start interrupting their behavior. (And remember to assess whether it's safe.)

Policies, Rules and Laws

When setting limits, it helps to avoid making it personal in situations where you can. Instead, try to refer to a policy, or rule, or law about the behavior that you're trying to set a limit on. Here's a few examples:

> *"I want to give you a heads up: When you take equipment home from our office it violates the company's policy and you risk getting fired. I encourage you not to do it. I'm just trying to help you out here."*

This often works better than just saying: "Don't do that!" This feels more personal and high-conflict people especially may take it as a personal attack and attack you back: "Who are you to tell me what I can and can't do?"

> *"The store is starting to set limits on people taking shopping carts away from the parking lot for their own personal use. There is a sign by the stop sign over there that says it violates the municipal code when you do that, which is a misdemeanor."*

This often works better than personally saying: "You can't do that!" Again, taking it personally, a high-conflict person might say "Mind your own business. Leave me alone."

> *"I'm sorry, but as a professional I'm not allowed to go to my client's houses for lunch. I am required by my ethical standards to maintain a strict boundary between my professional role and what friends might do. So, thanks for the invitation, but I am required to turn it down."*

This is certainly better than just saying: "I don't think that's a good idea." That can easily be taken as a personal rejection.

Getting Assistance

It can be hard to set limits on others, especially if they are very set in their ways or are difficult people. It can help to get assistance. If nothing else, find a good person to explain your situation to. Don't deal with it totally alone. At least talk to someone—almost anyone—so you don't feel isolated.

In many situations—family, workplace, organizations, community—there are policies that someone may be violating in their behavior toward you, especially against bullying and harassment. See if you can get some assistance in setting the limit and imposing consequences.

For example, there may be a respected authority figure in your family who you can talk to about someone else's behavior in the family (Grandma, Uncle Fred). They might be able to intervene on your behalf or at least give you some tips on how you can deal with this yourself. In the workplace there are managers, human resources, ombudsman, union reps, and so forth, who may be able to help you deal with the situation or at least give you some tips on how you can deal with it yourself.

In communities, there are community organizations, mediation centers, police community relations, religious organizations, court systems, therapists, and others available to help. Online there are lots of conflict resolution resources, consultants and coaches in a variety of settings who deal with difficult situations.

Keep in mind that there are millions of people dealing with difficult behavior, so that you are not alone and many people can empathize with what you are going through. With our inter-connected lives, there is often someone out there who understands and can help with your specific situation.

Conclusion

The first step of *SLIC Solutions* is to Set Limits. This means that you will need to speak up on your own behalf using the *assertive* approach (not too aggressive, not too passive). Remember the pointers from Chapter 1 about building up your confidence and practicing if necessary. Avoid letting the person argue with you and don't argue with them, it will sap your strength and may allow them to avoid the limit you set. Keep it simple and stay focused on what limit you are setting and do not get distracted. You don't need to justify yourself. Just say this is what you want or need, using "I" statements if you can (but no one is perfect about this).

You can try setting limits without mentioning any consequences and see what happens. Then, if that is insufficient (such as with high-conflict people who can't stop themselves), mention the consequence that you will impose if necessary. It needs to be a credible threat, so don't say something that you won't actually implement. That just teaches them that *all of your threats* of all consequences are probably empty and they may just escalate their negative behavior.

Anticipate push-back by thinking ahead about what they might say and what you can say in response—matter-of-factly—to stay focused on the limit you are setting. Remember that it is okay to interrupt someone's bad behavior or bad speech. It doesn't help anyone, especially high-conflict people, to go on and on blaming others while not taking any responsibility. You can interrupt them and state your limit with or without mentioning your consequences. In many situations it helps to get assistance in setting your limits so you will not be overpowered or talked out of it.

CHAPTER 3

STEP 2: IMPOSING CONSEQUENCES

If your limits are not respected, then it is appropriate to impose your consequences. This means that you should have thought through some potential consequences before you settled on what limit you are going to set. Impulsively setting limits and threatening extreme consequences is often ineffective and may undermine your future credibility for setting limits. Here are some questions to ask yourself to help you stop and think. We will explain each of these using a successful—and famous—example.

The Five Questions

1. ***Is the consequence proportional to the limit that I have set?***
2. ***Have I considered positive consequences as well as negative consequences?***
3. ***Is the consequence safe?***
4. ***Am I ready to enforce my consequence?***
5. ***Do I need to get help in imposing my consequence?***

As you will see, what is important is asking yourself these five questions. Sometimes it will be appropriate to say No instead of Yes, depending on the specifics of the situation. For example, it may not be appropriate to think of a positive consequence in some cases and you might not always need to get help in imposing your consequences.

To demonstrate imposing consequences, we are going to use Gerald's story—a true story that is one of the most famous examples of setting limits and imposing consequences with a substance abuse *intervention*. Gerald was Gerald Ford, former president of the United States (1974-1976). His pill-popping wife was Betty Ford, a beloved trailblazer who was active for many causes and brought public attention to her diagnosis and treatment of breast cancer—rarely discussed in public until she shared her personal story. However, after Gerald's term ended as president, she became more and more isolated, her alcohol and pill use increased, and her life was heading downhill fast.

It was their youngest adult daughter, Susan Ford, 20, who decided to do something about this. First, Susan, with Betty's personal assistant and a family doctor tried setting limits. They confronted her mother, as author Lisa McCubbin described in her 2018 book *Betty Ford: First Lady, Women's Advocate, Survivor, Trailblazer*:

"Mom, you need to stop taking all these pills," Susan told her. "I don't like what it's doing to you."

Betty Ford, then 59, was already under the influence of the pain medication she'd taken that morning and lashed out on the defensive. "You're all a bunch of monsters!" she shouted. "Get out of my house and never come back!" (loc 87 of 8445)

This first try is a good example of setting limits without realistic and proportional consequences ready. It failed miserably.

Susan then decided that she needed to get the whole family together to confront her mother, including her father and three brothers. They all needed to tell her to go into drug treatment. This was the limit she wanted to set. The positive consequence would be that the family would embrace her recovery. The negative consequence would be that they could not support her lifestyle and secret addiction. Let's examine this consequence with our five questions.

1. Is the consequence proportional to the limit I have set?

Setting the limit of going into a drug treatment was very appropriate and necessary but very hard with an addict who can't picture living without the drugs. Without stopping, she could eventually die from her pill addiction. Many people do. Therefore, even though the consequence of withdrawing all support for a beloved family member is extreme, it appears necessary and appropriate with an intervention. Susan also knew that pleading and being rational had not stopped her behavior and led to her rejecting her own daughter, personal assistant, and family doctor. A strong consequence was needed and family members were beginning to withdraw from her, including Susan's brother Jack who had already given up on his mother. At this point there was nothing left to lose by trying an intervention and her family needed to act quickly.

Yes, the consequence is proportional.

2. Have I considered positive consequences as well as negative consequences?

It often helps to point out that there are positive consequences to accepting the limit you have set as well as negative consequences for not following the limit. Susan planned to have each family member tell Betty that they wanted their prior, loving relationships back with her. Getting treatment for her pill addiction would bring back her happiness with all of them and her own happy life. This would be the positive consequence they would tell her if she accepted their limit of going into treatment.

Yes, they would present the positive consequences of following the limit as well as the obvious negative consequences if she did not.

3. Is the consequence safe?

While this question would seem to go without saying, it helps to address it because strong consequences sound appealing but may not always be safe. For example, threatening to expose someone's confidential information may put them in danger. Likewise, halting medical treatment or beating someone up as a consequence may be appealing, but very unsafe.

Yes, getting Betty into recovery would be the safest. If necessary, withdrawing family support for Betty's lifestyle would be less dangerous than her continued use of alcohol and drugs.

4. Am I ready to enforce my consequence?

To be really effective, it helps to think of all the possible arguments the person might make to dissuade you from enforcing your consequence. This way you can have all of your answers ready, at least in your own mind, to give you strength to follow through. It can also help to prepare yourself by practicing with someone else first. When it is clear that you are going to enforce your consequence, people may become more willing to accept your limit. In this case, Susan and her family met together beforehand to discuss what each person was going to say when they met with Betty. They decided the best order to go in and even wrote down what they would each say.

Yes, they were ready to enforce their consequences.

5. Will I need help in imposing my consequence?

Since bullies and other high-conflict people are often the ones who need limits set on them, it often takes more than one person to do this. They often ignore or overwhelm individuals setting limits, because they are more experienced at fighting than most people. In Betty's case, her dependency on the pills was stronger than the efforts of three people telling her to stop and she had already called all three of them "monsters." They needed more help, ideally from all of those closest to her.

Yes, in this case Susan sought the assistance of the whole immediate family and also a national expert on drug treatment and conducting interventions, a Navy physician, Dr. Joseph Pursch.

The Intervention

An "intervention" to get someone into alcohol and/or drug treatment was not developed until the 1970s. It involved everyone close to the person sharing a personal experience with the person's alcohol or drug use, and then insisting that they go into a treatment program. "Then they had to present her with consequences if she didn't agree." (loc 275 of 410)

With all of these five questions answered, let's see what actually happened on April 1, 1978:

Jerry Ford was the first to speak to his wife. "Betty," he said, "the reason we're here is because we love you."

Each child then spoke from the heart about their concern for their mom, who had become addicted to pain medication which had been prescribed by doctors for neck pain and arthritis, and which she had combined with alcohol.

"Mom, now you've got to the point where your lifestyle is destructive," her eldest, Mike Ford, told her. "It's hurting your relationship with Dad, with all of us, and with your friends..."

Her son Jack told his mom about the times he'd been embarrassed by her behavior. "I was always peeking around the corner into the family room to see what kind of shape you were in," he said. Their brother Steve followed.

At first, Betty was hurt — and angry, thinking to herself: "How dare they?"

Susan was shaking and crying as she said, "Mom, when I

was little, and even as I grew up, I always admired you for being a dancer. I wanted to be just like you. But now…these days, you're falling and you're clumsy. You're not the same person…" (loc 136 of 8445)

The intervention lasted for two hours. Dr. Pursch then asked Betty if she was willing to go into treatment, and she agreed.

This intervention and her drug and alcohol treatment was so successful, that Betty Ford stayed "clean and sober" for the rest of her life and established the Betty Ford centers for drug and alcohol treatment and other programs. Hundreds of thousands of people have become recovering alcoholics and addicts because of her programs, including many celebrities, since her family set limits on her and effectively threatened to impose their consequences–loss of family support.

Conclusion

There is a wide range of situations in which you will want to set limits and impose consequences, from simple parent-child daily management to complex interventions such as the one described here. Thinking through these five questions can help you slow down and become more effective in threatening realistic consequences when you set limits so that you don't have to actually impose the consequences. But if necessary you will need to be ready to do so. Betty Ford's family was ready to impose firm consequences if they needed to. If the wife of a President can have these problems and potentially need firm consequences, then anyone might.

CHAPTER 4

STEP 2½: EAR STATEMENT

(OR NOT - ABOUT HALF THE TIME)

When you set the limit and when you mention or impose consequences, in many situations it helps to add an *EAR Statement* which shows that you have *empathy, attention* and/or *respect* for the person on the receiving end. You can give the person an EAR Statement while you are setting the limit and/or when you are imposing your consequences. Any one or more of these three factors can serve as an EAR Statement, which only takes a few seconds to say or show.

An EAR Statement often helps the person accept the limit, helps keep your relationship positive, and helps them understand it's importance in terms of improving their behavior for the future. Such statements can help reduce resentments by showing the person that you have their best interests in mind as well as yours or those of your family, organization, or community.

However, many high-conflict people (HCPs) are used to people trying to set limits on them, so they are used to arguing back. If they appear to be highly manipulative or aggressive, then an EAR Statement would feed into their dynamics and you may be better off without giving one. This is the "half" step of SLIC Solutions: in about half of situations you give an EAR Statement and in the other half you are better off without including it to stay focused on the limit and the consequence.

EAR Statements

An EAR Statement can be this simple: "You can no longer come to my home if you are going to behave that way. I can understand that this may be frustrating or inconvenient or hard, but it is what I must do." By saying you "can understand" you are giving the person empathy even while setting the limit. Statements that start with "I can see or hear or understand that you might be feeling __________" show that you are treating the person as an equal because you *can* see it this way. This way you have empathy for them, rather than looking down on them by saying "I *can't* understand why you feel that way," which is what uninformed people often say around HCPs, which does not help.

For example, a parent might say to a child: "I'm telling you that if this happens again I will need to restrict you from going to that friend's house. This is because I love you and want to protect you from such potentially harmful situations." (Empathy)

Or a teacher might say: "I am setting this limit and I am willing to impose this consequence because I want to help you change this behavior. Do you have any questions for me about this? I want to understand any concerns you might have." (Attention)

Or a manager might say: "If you cover up your lack of progress on this project again, then I may have to end your employment here and I would really rather not do that. I respect you so much as a valued employee, but even we have limits." (Respect)

You can also show EAR Statements non-verbally, such as by having a friendly facial expression, calm tone of voice, and open body language. Avoid crossing your arms, looking away, rolling your eyes, etc. We have learned that your tone of voice is often the most important way in which to communicate empathy, attention, and respect. The exact words often matter less than showing your interest in them, that you have a caring attitude, and are not using a hostile posture while setting your limit and, if necessary, imposing your consequences.

Avoid Being Too Nice

It is a part of human nature for most, but not all, human beings to have empathy for each other. However, those who lack empathy are often high-conflict people who need to have limits set on them and in many cases consequences imposed. While you may still feel empathy for them because their behavior is so self-defeating, in some situations it is wiser to have *empathy at a distance* and not express it directly to them.

In these situations, EAR Statements fail to help or backfire. You need to avoid the trap of being too nice. Bullies and some other high-conflict people will try to dominate you and manipulate you if you give them an EAR Statement. In these situations, it's best to stay focused on firmly setting the limit and, if necessary, firmly imposing the consequences. The following are examples of how some people may attempt to manipulate you, so an EAR Statement would not be recommended:

> *"You said you cared about me and had empathy for me. How can you care about me and yet refuse to allow me to do _____? You're a hypocrite. I'm going to tell people that you really aren't the nice person you appear to be."*
>
> *"If you truly cared and paid attention to what I have told you, you would sign this paper here."*
>
> *"If you really respected me, you wouldn't insult me with this consequence. You're a little person and no one respects you."*

Rather than getting into such arguments and manipulations, skip the EAR Statement altogether if you anticipate such a response. Set your limit, impose your consequence if necessary, and then stand firm.

How Do You Know?

There is no clear-cut way to determine when to use an EAR Statement and when not to use one. It often is based on a gut feeling that the person wants to dominate or manipulate you. When in doubt, skip the EAR Statement. On the other hand, if you give an EAR Statement and the person pushes back, like the examples above, then stay focused on your limit and consequences and don't discuss or argue about your EAR Statement any further. Be prepared for such a response if you think the person might have a lack of empathy or remorse and will use your kind words against you. Don't get stuck defending yourself or your consequences. Just set your limit and impose your consequences.

If you are dealing with a bully, then you are facing someone who has a drive to dominate or destroy you and others. If you give a bully an EAR Statement, they will use it to put you down and dominate you—and try to wiggle out of the consequence. Therefore, it's better to be prepared and focus on setting your limits and imposing your consequences. Stand firm and get help if necessary. If you're dealing with a bully, it usually takes more than one person to stop them.

Strengthening Your Assertiveness

We often doubt ourselves, especially when someone is giving us such negative feedback. "What did I do to deserve this?" "I must not be very good at ______." "I have no right to ask the other person to change their behavior." But HCPs and bullies are generally not self-reflective. They are *pre-occupied* with blaming others, so that you may be experiencing their blame with no justification. You may have done nothing wrong. With bullies, you don't deserve to be bullied—no one does. It's their behavior that is the problem. You need to consider this possibility.

As nice people we often tell ourselves: "It's not nice to tell other people how to behave." "People will think we're bossy or nasty, if we tell them what to do or what not to do." However, when people are violating your boundaries or their behavior interferes with your life, you have the right to tell them to stop or change what they are doing. It is one of the most fundamental rights of assertiveness.

We also tend to have naïve beliefs that HCPs will stop themselves. "He'll come to his senses and stop doing this, I'm sure." "She'll realize that this behavior is inappropriate and even self-sabotaging." "I hope they get tired of treating me this way soon." This wishing and hoping doesn't work with HCPs. They lack the restraints to stop themselves. This self-talk doesn't help with HCPs and may keep you trapped in a bad situation.

We can change your self-talk. It's okay to ask yourself: "What's my part in this problem?" But then you need to consider asking yourself: "What's the other person's part in this problem?" Then, "It's okay to set limits with other people to protect ourselves." "And if they violate the limit, then it's okay to impose reasonable consequences." This doesn't make you a not-nice person. It just makes you an assertive person. In these tough situations where you are likely to get criticisms from an HCP, setting limits and imposing consequences without an EAR Statement is totally appropriate.

Example of Lending Money

Should Juanita include an EAR Statement or avoid it in the following example? Let's try it both ways and see how it works:

> *Juanita: "I can't lend you any more money because you haven't paid me back the money I lent you last month which you promised to repay in a few days."*

Jane: "Don't be a jerk. You know I'm in a difficult spot and need it more than you."

Juanita: "I'm sorry. I can understand that this is frustrating. [EAR Statement] But I really can't do it until you pay me back what I lent you before."

Jane: "You're not sorry! And you don't understand! If you were really sorry and really cared about me, you would lend me some more right now. You're not the nice person that people think you are!"

Juanita (caught off-guard and doesn't want to be seen as a not-nice person): "Well, okay. But this is the last time I'll do this."

By giving an EAR Statement to this particular Jane, Juanita set herself up for manipulation. First of all, saying "I'm sorry" implies that Juanita is doing something wrong by setting this limit. It puts her in a one-down position with a potentially high-conflict person. Apologies are great between most people, but with angry HCPs they will use it as ammunition against you (as Jane did here) and are best avoided. Secondly, saying "I understand" shows empathy, but again, Jane is going to try to use that empathy to manipulate Juanita by saying she is *not a nice person.* This is the type of situation where an EAR Statement is not recommended.

Let's try this situation again without an EAR Statement:

Juanita: "I can't lend you any more money because you haven't paid me back the money I lent you last month which you promised to repay in a few days."

Jane: "Don't be a jerk. You know I'm in a difficult spot and need it more than you.

Juanita: "As I said, I really can't do it until you pay me back what I lent you before."

Jane: "Come on. Please!"

Juanita: "You've heard me. This conversation is over. Was there something else you wanted to talk about?"

In this situation, Juanita didn't set herself up for manipulation and didn't get caught off-guard. She set the limit a month ago when she lent the money and she is imposing the consequence now by not lending any more until that is repaid. Juanita also kept it brief and then responded briefer and briefer when Jane argued back: First, saying "As I said..." Then, simply saying "You've heard me. This conversation is over." This is a good example of setting a limit, imposing a consequence, and standing firm.

Conclusion

SLIC solutions include an EAR Statement in many situations. It can be a short statement showing *empathy*, or that you will pay *attention* to their concerns, or that you *respect* something about them. This can help the person on the receiving end to accept your limit and, if necessary, your consequences. EAR also helps to maintain a positive relationship and to reinforce the importance of the desired behavior.

On the other hand, in other situations (perhaps half) when the person on the receiving end is domineering or manipulative it is better to skip the EAR Statement altogether and stay focused on setting the limit and firmly imposing the consequences. Avoid arguing about your SLIC solutions, just repeat what you have said once and then stop discussing it. Bullies and other high-conflict people often try to wiggle out of consequences, so be prepared for their arguments and be firm in your responses. Remember that EAR Statements are optional.

CHAPTER 5

FAMILY SITUATIONS

Setting limits is common and necessary in family situations. There are often several possible consequences, both negative and positive. In this chapter we will look at examples including couple relationships and parent-child situations. We will use the same basic structure for each example throughout the book. For a List of Examples, look in the back of the book.

Background

Step 1: Setting Limits
Step 2: Imposing Consequences (Including the Five Questions)
Step 2½: EAR Statement (or Not)

Discussion

Imagine this: it's a typical Tuesday evening. The scent of dinner still lingers, a moment of calm before the inevitable storm. Your teenager is testing limits, pushing back with an attitude sharpened by independence. Your young child is uncooperative at the most inconvenient times. Your partner has a different take on discipline, sparking yet another debate over parenting styles.

You love them all—deeply—but at times, it feels like love is a battlefield where personal space, respect, and sanity are constantly under siege.

Welcome to the intricate complex world of family and friendships, where the lines between love, support, and outright chaos often blur. Saying "no" feels like a betrayal; setting limits feels like building a wall, and pursuing harmony, too, often leads to silent resentment. You tell yourself it's easier to avoid conflict, keep the peace, and let things slide. But at what cost? How often do you feel emotionally drained, sacrificing your well-being to make others comfortable?

If you've ever felt like you're walking a tightrope—balancing between being a good parent or supportive partner—while your needs get pushed aside, you're not alone. The struggle to set and enforce limits is universal, shaped by unspoken family rules, cultural expectations, and the ever-present fear of being seen as selfish or unkind.

In this chapter, we'll dive headfirst into limit-setting—how "just a little advice" can morph into control, how guilt is often used as a leash, and how subtle manipulations can make us question our right to say no. Most importantly, we'll equip you with the tools to navigate this complex terrain with confidence and compassion. Because at the end of the day, setting limits isn't about shutting people out—it's about creating space for relationships to thrive.

TEENAGE SON – GAMING

Background

In early 2025, the Williams family—Linda, a single mother, her son Jake, and her elderly parents—faced a growing challenge. Linda was contacted by Jake's teacher about declining grades and suspected plagiarism. She had already noticed Jake prioritizing video games over homework, leading to academic decline and tension at home.

Jake had started using AI tools to complete assignments, which the teacher and Linda viewed as dishonest. Despite her repeated efforts to set limits, Jake dismissed her concerns, insisting that using AI was normal. Their conversations became increasingly strained as Jake resisted her rules and continued gaming.

One day Linda confronted Jake in their living room about his continued gaming and incomplete homework. Jake admitted to using AI for assignments, but downplayed the seriousness, calling it modern technology. Linda pushed back, stressing that it's unethical and undermines his learning.

These behaviors were harming Jake's academic performance and straining his relationship with Linda. To rebuild trust and responsibility, Linda must set clear limits and follow through with appropriate consequences.

Step 1: Setting Limits

Linda calmly and firmly set her limits: "Jake, you must complete your homework before playing video games or using AI tools for assignments. You'll focus on your work first, and then you can enjoy gaming once your tasks are finished. If you find it challenging to manage both, let's discuss a schedule to help balance things. Let me know if you need help staying on track. No more game-playing before your assignments are completed."

Linda thought to herself why this limit might work: It addresses Jake's problematic behaviors directly. It establishes a fair system where Jake earns gaming time by completing his work. But she also thought to herself why this limit might not work: Jake might find ways to circumvent the rules, such as secretly playing games or lying about completing homework. He could push back emotionally, feeling restricted or micromanaged, leading to further arguments. She knew that she might struggle to enforce the limit consistently, undermining her own authority. She thought ahead about what her consequences would be if her limits were not followed.

Step 2: Imposing Consequences

If Jake disregards Linda's limit, she decided that she would use consequences such as the following to reinforce the seriousness of her request. These consequences would support his responsibility while reinforcing respect for the household rules.

- Limit Access to Electronics: Restrict access to the gaming console or disable the Wi-Fi for the evening, ensuring that homework remains the priority.

- Require Homework Completion Before Privileges: Reinstate gaming privileges only after Jake has demonstrated responsibility by completing assignments.

- Meet with the Teacher: If Jake continues to misuse AI dishonestly, Linda can contact his teacher to develop a plan for accountability and require Jake to redo the assignment.

- Establish a Study Routine: Implement a structured homework schedule where Jake completes assignments in a designated space before earning screen time.

As it turned out, the day after Linda set her limit of homework first, Jake automatically started playing his video games when he got home from school and was still playing them when Linda got home from work. She gave him one reminder, telling him that if he continued playing before getting his assignments done, she would turn off the Wi-Fi until they were done. But after this reminder with a threat of consequences, he still ignored her. He couldn't stop himself. So, Linda disabled the Wi-Fi until he finished his assignments.

How did she answer the Five Questions?

1. ***Is the consequence proportional to the limit that I have set?***

Yes! Just disabling the Wi-Fi until the homework is done is a logical fit for the limit she set.

2. ***Have I considered positive consequences as well as negative consequences?***
   Yes, she emphasized how this will help him learn responsibility for his future success.
3. ***Is the consequence safe?***
   Yes! Turning off the Wi-Fi is certainly safe.
4. ***Am I ready to enforce my consequence?***
   Yes! She thought it through and was ready with her consequence if it became necessary and followed through.
5. ***Do I need to get help in imposing my consequence?***
   Possibly. If necessary, she would meet with Jake's teacher to develop a plan.

Step 2½: EAR Statement (or Not)

Linda decided that an EAR Statement (showing *empathy, attention, and/or respect*) could help Jake without weakening the enforcement of her limits by acknowledging his feelings and giving him some empathy.

"I can understand that you want to play video games, but these rules exist to help you succeed. I know school is stressful, and you need a break. But before I'm home you need to start working on your schoolwork. I'm here to support you, but I can't let you avoid your responsibilities."

Jake was about to argue with her, but after her EAR Statement he just silently switched to his schoolwork. After this consequence, he started his homework before she walked through the door after work each day. She didn't need to do it again.

She also told him that if she heard that he was improperly using AI to do his assignments, that she would need to meet with him and his teacher about it. As far as she knew, he stopped doing that. She didn't hear further from his teacher about that.

Discussion

This case illustrates the need for clear limits when a child's behavior affects academic performance. While Jake seeks independence, Linda must ensure his gaming habits don't interfere with his responsibilities. Setting limits and imposing consequences helped him build accountability. While Jake pushed back, feeling controlled and misunderstood, Linda was able to balance firmness with empathy. By validating his emotions while upholding consistent rules, she kept communication open and reinforced responsibility. Her approach supported not only Jake's current academic needs but also fostering skills like honesty, time management, and prioritization.

In looking at the steps Linda took in this case, she started out by setting her limit (homework first) without threatening or imposing any consequences. As often happens, this didn't work. Then she threatened a consequence (turning off the Wi-Fi), but this also didn't work. What finally worked was to impose the consequence of turning off the Wi-Fi. She only had to do this once.

This was also a case where an EAR Statement was highly appropriate. With children it is especially important to connect the dots of their behavior to future success. She let Jake know that she cared about him and that following the household rules and learning responsibility would help him for years to come. Over time, this balanced strategy will lead to stronger academic habits and essential life skills, ensuring Jake's development both in school and beyond.

TEENAGE DAUGHTER – LYING

Background

In early 2025, the Martinez family was tangled in serious incidents surrounding trust and privacy. Teenage daughter Isabel had been lying about her after-school activities. While her parents believed she was attending a study group at a friend's house, she was actually meeting up with a new group of friends she had met online. This group often engaged in activities that her parents would disapprove of, such as skipping school and attending unofficial parties.

When confronted by her parents, Ana and Marco, about her whereabouts one afternoon, Isabel defensively claimed she was at the library studying, which was later proven false by her mother's discovery of social media posts from that day showing her at a local park with her new friends. This pattern of deception continued, with Isabel fabricating elaborate stories to conceal her real activities, effectively betraying her parents' trust despite their efforts to encourage open communication. Her lies not only created a rift between her and her parents but also sparked deeper questions about her judgment and the influences around her.

One night, after dinner in the Martinez family living room, the following discussion took place:

Ana: "Isabel, we've noticed you've been going out after school without telling us. What's going on?"

Isabel: "Mom, it's no big deal. I was hanging out with friends."

Ana: "Isabel, you told us you were staying after school for study sessions. You've been lying to us, and that's not okay. We have rules in this house."

Marco: "We've trusted you, Isabel. How can we trust you when you keep sneaking around? This isn't just about where you're going; it's about respect for our trust."

Isabel: "You guys are overreacting. I'm not a kid anymore! Why do you keep trying to control everything I do?"

Ana: "It's not about control but being honest with us. Keeping our relationship strong is hard if we can't trust you."

Marco: "Lying isn't acceptable. You've already missed two assignments this week. Your grades have dropped. We need to set clearer limits."

Isabel: "This is so unfair! I need my space, but you guys just don't get it."

Ana: "We understand you need space, but you must be honest with us about where you're going and with whom."

There are several problematic behaviors here that make the parents consider setting limits:

Lying: Isabelle deceives her parents about her whereabouts after school. Their trust in her is undermined.

Dismissiveness: Isabel dismisses her parents' concerns and minimizes the seriousness of the situation.

Defensiveness: Isabel becomes defensive and frustrated instead of acknowledging her actions, escalating the tension.

Lack of Respect for Rules: Isabel disregards the family rules regarding honesty and communication.

Parental Concern Ignored: Ana and Marco's concerns about Isabel's safety and the integrity of their relationship are brushed aside.

Step 1: Setting Limits

The parents agreed that Ana would have a talk with Isabel to set their limits.

Ana (calmly and assertively): "Isabel, we need to have trust in our family. Starting now, we need you to be completely honest about where you're going and who you're with. If you feel uncomfortable sharing that information, let's talk about it together. However, if we find out that you're still lying to us, we will need to discuss some consequences for that behavior. We want to support you, but honesty is key."

Ana and Marco thought about why this might work: They communicated their limits and what is expected of Isabel. The limit directly addresses the core issue—dishonesty. Consistency: Setting a firm limit helps restore consistency in their relationship.

They also considered why it might not work: Isabel is a teenager and testing limits comes with the territory. She may resist the new rule, believing that it infringes on her independence. She might continue to lie or become more secretive, testing her parents' limits. Ana and Marco may struggle to enforce the limits consistently, leading to potential arguments or further rebellion.

Ana and Marco agreed that if setting the limit alone doesn't work, then they will need to set the limit and state the specific consequence if the limit is not followed.

Step 2: Impose the Consequence

A few days after Ana and Isabel's talk about limits, Ana found out that Isabel went to a boy's house right after school with two other friends the parents didn't know. No adults were there at that time. Ana and Marco were furious, but they calmed down and discussed what the consequence should be. They presented this together to Isabel.

Marco said: "We are concerned about your health and safety after school. Therefore, we need to impose a realistic consequence for your risk-taking behavior. We have asked around and found out that the boy whose house you went to has been in trouble at the school for truancy and drugs. So you are forbidden to go there. But at your age making your own friends is important, so you should feel free to bring them over to our house after school. After all, Ana is working from home now.

"But that just takes care of your safety. You also lied to us again, after we told you there would be consequences for that. So you are grounded for this weekend—you'll need to stay at home—and we are taking your cell phone away for 24 hours. This will give you time to think about the importance of being honest with us.

Ana added: "If this happens again, then we will take you to a counselor who works a lot with teenagers. We hear that this counselor likes to have the teen write an essay about the risks of hanging out with kids who get into trouble and lying to your parents, and what you could do instead to have a healthy and fun social life. But we'll see if that will be necessary. Do you have any questions about this?"

Isabel looked resigned and had no questions. She just said: "Fine, whatever. This is stupid."

How did Ana and Marco answer the Five Questions?

1. ***Is the consequence proportional to the limit that I have set?***
   Yes! Restricting her for one weekend and taking the phone away for 24 hours is not too severe given her risk-taking behavior.
2. ***Have I considered positive consequences as well as negative consequences?***
   Yes, they encouraged her to bring friends to their house where Ana could be home.
3. ***Is the consequence safe?***
   Yes! Keeping Isabel at home one weekend and without a phone for 24 hours should be very safe.
4. ***Am I ready to enforce my consequence?***
   Yes! Ana and Marco talked it over before meeting with Isabel, so they were ready to follow through.
5. ***Do I need to get help in imposing my consequence?***
   Yes! Ana and Marco helped each other, which made it much easier to be firm and present a united front.

Step 2½: EAR Statement (or Not)

In this case, EAR Statements are very important, so that the teenager feels cared for and understands the long-term benefits of following her parents' rules. With this in mind, Ana added the following:

Ana: "Isabel, I understand you feel like we're controlling you, and it feels harsh and unfair. (Empathy) I can see you're really frustrated right now. (Attention) We respect that you need space, and we want to find a safe way to make that work. (Respect)"

Marco added: "And it seems like you were just trying to have some fun with your friends, and that is something that is normal for teens. (Empathy) I am listening to what you are saying. (Attention) I respect the fact that you want to have friends and a social life. (Respect) Even though it may not feel like it now, protecting you from other risk-taking students will help your life be happier and more successful in the long run."

Using empathetic language helps convey care while still being firm about the consequences. This approach not only reinforces the limits but also encourages reflection and growth.

Discussion

The Martinez family case study illustrates a common struggle: the clash between adolescent rebellion and parental concern, complicated by a breakdown in communication and trust. At the core of the issue is Isabel's repeated dishonesty, which has severely damaged the family's trust; her parents' feelings of betrayal are entirely understandable. This situation also highlights the tension between a teenager's need for independence and a parent's responsibility to ensure their child's safety. While Isabel's desire for autonomy is typical of her age, her methods have created significant problems. The family's communication is hampered by defensiveness, with conversations quickly escalating into arguments rather than productive exchanges. Furthermore, the influence of Isabel's new peer group raises concerns about potential risks, and the parents struggle to set and enforce limits effectively without further alienating their daughter.

Ana and Marco's initial confrontation of setting limits, while direct, quickly became unproductive, and their focus on rules alone may not be sufficient. While setting limits is a positive step, its success depends on consistent enforcement with consequences while maintaining a supportive relationship.

Their use of EAR Statements should significantly improve their communication. To resolve these issues, the family needed to establish a safe space for open and honest dialogue, requiring active listening and empathy. They did a good job of this. Rebuilding trust will require time and consistent honesty from Isabel, along with forgiveness from her parents.

Exploring the underlying reasons for Isabel's behavior, such as peer pressure or feelings of inadequacy, is crucial. If they cannot resolve these issues independently, professional help may be necessary

Although Isabel pushed back at first, her parents are committed to staying consistent with their limits. This will encourage open conversations and mutual respect over time. Ultimately, their journey is all about finding discipline while creating a loving environment for healthy communication in the family. With a bit of patience, they can work towards a stronger and more trusting relationship!

As a separate matter, this was a good example of a couple working closely together on solving a problem. Not all couples are this cooperative with each other. The following example shows setting limits and imposing consequences in a more difficult relationship.

COUPLE IN CONFLICT – FEELING TRAPPED

Background

Maya, a passionate fashion designer thriving in Los Angeles, was swept off her feet by Alessandro, a charming banker with an adventurous spirit. From the moment they met, Maya was convinced he was her soulmate. As their relationship blossomed, she began to notice a troubling pattern.

When her company sent her on trips, Alessandro would eagerly tag along. But he mostly focused on his own experiences while ignoring Maya. Even more unsettling were the moments when Alessandro would playfully pinch Maya's arms, his laughter ringing hollow as bruises formed in places usually concealed beneath clothing. He brushed it off with a wave whenever she brought up her discomfort, dismissing it as harmless fun.

Maya traveled to Canada for work one day, and Alessandro came along. When they arrived, he took a small bag from her luggage. Maya asked, "What is that?" He replied, "It's marijuana; you can use it if you're anxious about traveling." Maya was so shocked that she screamed, "First of all, I do not use it! And it's illegal to fly across the border with this into Canada, and you put it into my luggage, making it seem like I bought it. I can go to jail for it." But he just laughed, either not understanding or not caring about how serious his actions were.

One day, Alessandro (the banker) bluntly said he could never marry someone with debt. At the time, Maya was struggling with her student loans. He insisted that a partner should have at least $25,000 in savings. To prove his point, he opened his personal laptop, logged into his Bank work account, and showed a profile of multiple women from Maya's cultural background who had that amount in high-yield savings accounts. Maya felt manipulated as her autonomy was undermined, and anxiety rose about her future.

After two years of living together, Maya's relationship with Alessandro was far from the fairytale she had imagined. Alessandro used careful words and subtle insults to weaken her confidence and independence. This left Maya questioning her worth as the relationship became more one-sided.

Step 1: Setting Limits

Throughout the relationship, Maya attempted to set limits.

Privacy limits: "What you did by sneaking marijuana, a drug illegal to transport to Canada, in my luggage is a huge violation of my trust and has legal implications. If you ever put anything in my belongings without my consent again, I will no longer allow you to travel with me. I cannot risk my safety or my future because of your recklessness." After that, he never did something that extreme again.

Physical limits: "I am not comfortable with being pinched in that way. If it happens again, I will ask you to leave." But it happened again in small ways and she didn't leave.

Emotional limits: "I need to be treated respectfully when I express my feelings. If you dismiss or belittle my concerns, I will walk away from the conversation." But usually she didn't.

In abusive relationships, setting limits can be an important first step, but they are often not enough to stop the cycle of abuse. This is especially true when dealing with someone like Alessandro, who has shown a pattern of manipulation, control, and disregard for limits

Step 2: Imposing Consequences

The last straw came when Maya found out that Alessandro was seeing another woman. It became clear that their problems were never going to end and that Alessandro was never going to change. While she blamed herself for not being firmer with the limits that she set, Maya decided that the only way forward for her life was to leave him. This would be the ultimate consequence for his behavior. But she was afraid of what he might do if she confronted him. Simply telling an abuser "no" or "stop" is often met with retaliation, escalation, or manipulation. She had heard that when a partner is physically abusive one of the most dangerous times is when the woman tries to leave him.

Maya decided that she needed support and safety. She spoke to a friend who referred her to a therapist familiar with abusive relationships. After a few sessions, she was ready to leave. She also went to a restraining order clinic that helped people get court orders of protection if necessary. If he became threatening, then she was prepared to get an order keeping him 100 yards away from her.

She decided to move all of her belongings out of their place when Alessandro was away for a weekend, possibly with the other woman. Then she left him a short note explaining the decision she had come to and that she would help pay the rent for two more months if he didn't bother her.

How did Maya answer the Five Questions?

1. ***Is the consequence proportional to the limit that I have set?***
   Yes! Safety first!
2. ***Have I considered positive consequences as well as negative consequences?***
   Yes, she would pay two more months' rent if he let her go in peace.
3. ***Is the consequence safe?***
   Yes! She is not physically present when he gets the news.
4. ***Am I ready to enforce my consequence?***
   Yes! She got ready with help from her therapist.
5. ***Do I need to get help in imposing my consequence?***
   Yes! She got help from friends in moving her belongings out of the apartment.

Step 2½: EAR Statement (or Not)

Maya knew Alessandro would call her in anger after seeing that she had left. She was tempted to tell him that it was all her fault to calm him down, blaming herself because she wasn't strong enough to stick up for herself in the relationship. But her therapist helped her understand that in abusive dynamics, the abuser often thrives on controlling and manipulating their partner. Using empathy to understand their perspective, paying attention to their needs, or respecting their views might unintentionally validate the abuser's harmful actions and make them feel justified in their abusive behavior.

Fortunately, he just yelled at her over the phone that it was all her fault and that she would miss out on his coming financial success. He insulted her and said he wanted nothing to do with her. He had already moved on to his new relationship. Instead of giving him an EAR Statement, she let him blame her without responding. She would get her support and validation from others, not him. He mostly stayed away and she was free.

Discussion

Setting limits and imposing consequences can be tricky in a case of domestic violence and needs to be done very carefully. While the violence (pinching) may have seemed minor in this case, it did leave bruises and he didn't stop. He also showed signs of "coercive control," in that he freely put illegal drugs in her luggage and belittled her concerns. Any level of violence is usually related to efforts to control the other person's activities, which often includes who they associate with, where they go, how they spend their time, how they manage money, what they eat, and how they relate to the abuser. Setting limits and imposing consequences is hard in these situations because most abusers don't stop themselves. That's why the courts have to issue so many restraining orders.

Imposing consequences with an abusive person can easily run the risk of violence in response. "How dare you!" In this case, Maya was wise to get some help in preparing to leave in a safe way. Often just telling an abusive person that you want to leave or end the relationship can be life-threatening. That's why she was wise not to be physically present when Alessandro got the news. If that wasn't possible, then having someone else with her would have been advised. Being ready to get a restraining order was a good idea, although it didn't turn out to be necessary.

An important point about this case is that Maya didn't tell Alessandro her consequence before leaving. She acted on it instead. While she suggested that the relationship would be in trouble if his behavior didn't change, she never followed through before. The reality is that imposing consequences can be done without warning if safety is involved. Some people consider this a form of "silent consequences," such as when you just walk away from a conversation without explaining yourself because the other person is being so disgusting or threatening. When it became clear to her that Alessandro was not going to change after two years, she was no longer trying to influence his behavior but rather trying to get away from it all together.

This case reveals both overt and subtle forms of emotional abuse. Alessandro used covert manipulation to undermine Maya's autonomy and self-worth. Unlike physical violence, psychological abuse is harder to identify but equally harmful. Maya feels pressured to empathize with Alessandro despite his hurtful actions, leading to internal conflict and self-doubt—a common effect of emotional manipulation.

Alessandro's dismissiveness, such as mocking her concerns about the drug or the bruising on her arms, invalidates her emotions and deepens the power imbalance. As a result, Maya may start questioning her own perceptions and feel isolated or responsible for his behavior.

Victims of emotional abuse often struggle to set limits without external support. Trusted friends, counselors, or support groups can help Maya gain perspective, recognize manipulation, and reclaim her sense of agency. Emotional bonds, gaslighting, and hope for change make it difficult for victims to leave—even when abuse is clear.

To heal, Maya must define her worth independently of Alessandro. Therapy or personal reflection (through journaling, art, etc.) can help rebuild her confidence, assert her needs, and untangle manipulation from reality. It also allows her to explore deeper reasons for staying, such as fear of abandonment or codependency.

In a non-violent couple relationship, it is not unusual to set limits on problematic behavior and, if necessary, to impose the consequence of going to couples counseling for several sessions to try to improve the relationship. This is a logical consequence for couples having difficulty. However, if the partner won't go to counseling, then that's a sign that things won't improve and the consequence may be ending the relationship.

Conclusion

This chapter covered a range of family conflicts. With teenagers it is common to have these types of limit setting situations. With abusive adult partner relationships, it is less common, but still widespread enough that everyone should learn about the warning signs of abuse and how to set limits within the relationship or how to get out.

Three Key SLIC Lessons that fit for all of these situations:

1. ***Clarity:*** Make it clear what the behavior was and what the consequence will be.
2. ***Consistency:*** Stick to your consequences if the behavior continues.

3. ***Protect yourself:*** If the behavior is severe, like in cases of abuse or danger, don't hesitate to distance yourself, involve others, or take legal action to protect yourself.

If you or someone you know is experiencing domestic abuse, please reach out for help. You can contact the National Domestic Violence Hotline at 800-799-7233 or visit their website at: **https://www.thehotline.org/get-help/**

CHAPTER 6

DIVORCE SITUATIONS

Divorce (and separation of unmarried couples) is a very common situation today, as 40-50 percent of couples end their relationships in separation or divorce. This presents many opportunities for conflict and the need for setting limits. So we have a separate chapter on this subject with two types of examples, in-court and out-of-court. The vast majority, perhaps 80%, of divorces are resolved out of court by agreement of the spouses.

However, since people with *high-conflict* personalities are frequently involved in interpersonal disputes, it is not surprising that there are a lot of *high-conflict* people involved in family court cases. Perhaps half of the 20% of divorce cases that end up in court have *high-conflict* situations that can go on for months or years, because it is hard to tell what is occurring (he said/she said) or one party refuses to follow court orders. In those cases, family courts are necessary for setting limits and imposing consequences, such as for interference with the other parent's time with the child or for nonpayment of child support.

This chapter includes three examples of setting limits and imposing consequences in these cases. One about parenting time, one about an unpaid financial payment, and one about handling a conflict after the divorce.

GETTING CHILD LATE TO SCHOOL

Background

Oscar loved his 8-year-old daughter, Emily, and he loved to teach her things. But the mother, Sally, showed the court evidence that he had a problem getting her to school on time in the mornings. During the parents' divorce, the family court judge ordered a parenting schedule with equally shared parenting time over the objection of the mother. Every week she had responsibility on Mondays and Tuesdays after school including overnights and back to school the next day, and he had Wednesdays and Thursdays after school including overnights and back to school the next day. They would alternate Fridays through Sundays.

Step 1: Setting Limits

The judge set limits as follows: "Sir, I have heard the mother's objections to this shared parenting schedule, but I trust that you will get your daughter to school on time from now on. Can you assure me that you can do that?"

"Yes, your honor," Oscar replied. "No problem."

The judge continued: "If you do have difficulty getting her to school on time, then I may have to reduce the number of school days from your parenting time. Is that clear?"

"Yes, your honor," Oscar replied again. "No problem."

The judge felt confident that his verbal admonishment might be enough, but he was ready to impose the consequence of reducing Oscar's parenting time if necessary.

Step 2: Imposing Consequences

Unfortunately, Oscar failed to follow the judge's admonishment about getting Emily to school on time. Therefore, Sally filed a court motion three months after the divorce was finalized asking for a modification of the parenting schedule. She submitted a schedule from the school showing how often Emily was late. All of the late days were during his parenting time.

Back at court, would the judge actually impose consequences?

"Sir," the judge said. "I'd like to understand these late days. Tell me what's going on. There are six of them in three months. That's not good."

Oscar replied: "I'm very responsible and always drive Emily to school on my parenting days. I get there early and then spend the free time teaching her vocabulary and multiplication tables in the car. I know sometimes I got preoccupied and got her into the school late, but since I'm personally teaching her she's learning a lot. But it won't happen again."

The judge responded: "Actually, I am going to order a change in the parenting schedule. I'm going to stop your Wednesdays overnight with her, so that you will not be responsible for taking her to school on Thursday mornings. However, you will still have Thursday evenings to help her with her homework and Friday mornings to get her to school on time, as well as alternate Monday mornings when it's your weekend."

How did the judge answer the Five Questions?

1. ***Is the consequence proportional to the limit that I have set?***
   Yes. Oscar was just reduced by one day each week. Some would argue this was too big of a consequence, but he was warned it could happen.
2. ***Have I considered positive consequences as well as negative consequences?***
   Yes. Oscar still has his other parenting time and if he

improves his school drop-offs it could help him in future parenting plans.

3. ***Is the consequence safe?***
   Yes.
4. ***Am I ready to enforce my consequence?***
   Yes. Especially since the judge gave a prior warning, the judge was ready to impose the new parenting order.
5. ***Do I need to get help in imposing my consequence?***
   No. It's a court order.

Step 2½: EAR Statement (or Not)

In this case, the judge believed that an EAR Statement would be helpful because Oscar seemed so sincere. Since the goal was to improve his behavior, an EAR Statement might help.

The judge continued: "I can understand that this is not what you wanted. But the circumstances indicate to me that this is a hard habit for you to break. We are beyond promises to do better since this was a problem before and I gave you a chance. I made it very clear that I might change the parenting schedule if a problem continued. While I respect your efforts to teach your daughter, it is also important to teach timeliness and responsibility. I hope that this will not be a problem in the future. I wish both of you all the best."

Discussion

This is a good example of using the courts to hold people accountable and to impose consequences when needed. Setting limits was appropriate because of the prior problem with Oscar's tardiness. The judge was right that this was a "hard habit to break" for Oscar. Such habits don't usually change unless there is an attention-getting consequence. This is what seemed to happen here. This is based on a real case, but the outcome is unknown. In the future, it would seem that Oscar would be more successful on the school mornings that he had remaining after experiencing this painful consequence. Sadly, behavior change often requires painful consequences.

The judge's EAR Statement seemed very appropriate and Oscar seemed touched by it, even though he wanted to argue with the judge. The judge made clear it wasn't negotiable, but did it with empathy ("I can understand…"), attention ("tell me what's going on"), and respect ("I respect your efforts…").

Family courts are not a good place to make parenting decisions, but sometimes they are needed to set limits and impose consequences. The preparations for a hearing require information to be provided by the parties, which means that they often say upsetting things about each other in the papers that they file and exchange a few days before the hearing. The outcome is often uncertain, as judges are busy making the initial divorce decisions and setting limits at the same time. Many do not have the time to address issues and impose consequences after the divorce because their schedules are so full. Yet that is sometimes necessary, as in this case.

UNPAID EQUALIZING PAYMENT

Background

Jennifer's ex-husband, Jason, owes her a $10,000 equalizing payment from their divorce settlement agreement. It's been two years since he was supposed to pay it and she still hasn't seen any of it. He keeps saying he'll get around to it, but he doesn't take any action to make it happen. He has a higher income and can afford it, but he just won't. Should she go to court? Or will that just make him angrier and more resistant? Will the court even enforce its own orders?

The lawyer who helped Jennifer reach a full Marital Settlement Agreement with her ex has retired. So, Jennifer discussed her options with another family law attorney. She suggested a few steps for Jennifer:

"Obviously, Jason is not going to pay you unless there is some kind of consequence hanging over his head. I suggest that we file for a court hearing to enforce this debt with an order that you can take to his employer or to his bank which requires that they pay you directly. It's called a Money Judgment and it requires a court order beyond the terms that you already have in your Marital Settlement Agreement. But after we file for the hearing, I suggest that when we send him the notice of the hearing that you agree to a voluntary payment plan with deadlines that have to be met in order to avoid having to actually have that hearing. We can hold it over his head as a consequence if he doesn't follow through. Often people want to avoid going to court, so that might motivate him. We can postpone the hearing for a while, but as soon as he misses a deadline the hearing will happen."

Jennifer said: "I like that idea. I just think he needs some motivation to make the payment. Right now there has been no consequence beyond me complaining to him about it. That hasn't worked."

Step 1: Setting Limits

Jennifer and her lawyer filed for the court hearing, which would be in a month. The lawyer had a "process server" personally hand the hearing papers to Jason with a letter which said:

"I am the lawyer for Jennifer for this hearing. You will notice that the hearing is in one month. Jennifer has told me that she would prefer to settle this matter with a payment plan and deadlines that would make the hearing unnecessary, unless the payment plan is not followed. She proposes that you pay $3000 per month for the next three months (for a total of $9000), starting the first day of next month. We will postpone the hearing by a month each time a payment is received on time. This means that you will actually save $1000 by following through with this plan and making the hearing unnecessary.

"But if you miss a payment or don't agree to this payment plan (unless you make another proposal that Jennifer agrees to), then we will go forward with the hearing. When the judge makes the order, it will include interest on the unpaid amount, so it will be more than $10,000 total. We hope that won't be necessary. We prefer to keep this as amicable as possible. Please feel free to discuss this with a lawyer of your choice."

Step 2: Imposing Consequences

If Jason did not immediately pay $10,000 or $9,000, then Jennifer's consequence system would go into effect. It might motivate a settlement like the three-month plan, or it might require the full court hearing and imposing the Money Judgment on his income and accounts.

How did Jennifer answer the Five Questions?

1. ***Is the consequence proportional to the limit that I have set?***
   Yes. In fact, it's very generous since Jason was already two years overdue.
2. ***Have I considered positive consequences as well as negative consequences?***
   Yes. Jason gets a discount if he fulfills her three-month payment system.
3. ***Is the consequence safe?***
   Yes. Even if Jason is angry about this, Jennifer doesn't have to see him for the payments to be made and she has a lawyer as a buffer to deal directly with him instead of herself.
4. ***Am I ready to enforce my consequence?***
   Yes, especially since she has a lawyer helping her.
5. ***Do I need to get help in imposing my consequence?***
   Yes, the lawyer.

Outcome: Will Jason pay Jennifer according to the proposal in the lawyer's letter? It depends on whether Jason is a high-conflict person who wants to fight about it or someone who doesn't want to deal with the hassle and will just pay her. Different cases like this have a wide range of outcomes, such as the following:

A. Avoidant, but generally reasonable Jason:

In this case, Jason agrees to the idea of a payment plan, signs the agreement and makes the three payments on schedule. The hearing is then taken off-calendar at the court. The consequence of a court hearing hanging over his head worked. True, Jennifer got less than she deserved, but she saved the cost of paying her lawyer to prepare for and attend the hearing (which could have been $1000).

B. Resistant Jason, but this approach worked:

This Jason would not agree to the payment plan and went to the court hearing complaining that he didn't have the money to pay Jennifer. He needed his salary for monthly expenses and his bank balance for emergencies. Jennifer's lawyer explained that he had a bank account balance of $5000 and that he got paid a decent salary at his job. If he had made payments starting two years ago, it would have been paid off by now. The court ordered the Money Judgment and the lawyer got the bank to pay the $5000 balance to Jennifer and the rest was paid to Jennifer over the next two years from his monthly wages. Unfortunately, this cost Jennifer about $2000, so she only ended up with $8000. But at least she got paid that.

C. Totally high-conflict Jason:

This Jason quit his job and withdrew all of his savings so that Jennifer could not reach them even with a court order. Some of the most high-conflict people will do anything to avoid responsibility. This is a hard reality in some of the most high-conflict cases. Fortunately, Jennifer and Jason did not have any children together, so this outcome—while very frustrating—does not have to ruin her life.

Step 2½: EAR Statement (or Not)

In this case there is no strong reason to give an EAR Statement, but since they are not dealing with each other directly, it can't hurt for Jennifer's lawyer to include a little empathy, attention or respect. She said "We hope that won't be necessary. We prefer to keep this as amicable as possible." These statements show a little bit of empathy for him and are probably sufficient, especially because he appears to be resistant to being responsible and presenting a firm limit makes the most sense.

Discussion

This case shows a common issue in divorces, especially high-conflict divorces. While family courts make a lot of orders during the divorce process, they don't usually need to manage enforcement of their orders. Most people simply follow them and move on in their lives. However, if necessary, there are enforcement mechanisms that family lawyers should consider when negotiating settlements and when asking for court orders in cases of resistant parties. People divorcing a high-conflict person should ask about these options from the start of their case.

STRONGER LIMITS AFTER DIVORCE

Sometimes the worst divorce battles occur after the divorce, because high-conflict behavior lives on. This example demonstrates efforts at positive consequences to influence behavior, but also the necessity of negative consequences.

Background

William got divorced three years ago. It was an amicable divorce and he still worked on his ex-wife's car as a favor, since he was a mechanic and it always needed work. However, when his new girlfriend moved in with him a couple months ago, Connie started interfering with his parenting time and began dropping by William's house uninvited. She convinced their 18-year-old daughter, who lived with him, to spy on him and his girlfriend and tell her everything about her. The daughter also invited strangers into their home, which William would not tolerate.

Connie had primary parenting time with their son, age 11, and William had alternate weekends and Wednesdays overnight. However, after William's girlfriend moved in, Connie started blocking William's contact with their son. His son wants to see him, but doesn't want to make his mother angry, so when William comes to the door he says that he doesn't want to go.

Step 1: Setting Limits

William told Connie that he was not going to work on her car anymore if she didn't stop dropping in on him at his house. He also told her he would go to the police to enforce their parenting schedule in the court order. Connie said "I don't care" to both of these limits.

He told their daughter that if she didn't leave his girlfriend alone or try to get along with her, then he would kick her out of his house and send her back to her mother, who kicked her out two years earlier.

Nothing worked to get Connie to leave him and his new girlfriend alone.

Step 2: Imposing Consequences

William decided to take action. He told his daughter to move back with her mother and she did. He stopped doing any work on Connie's car. After two months of not seeing his son, William finally went to the police with his court order showing his parenting time. A police officer went with him to Connie's house and said she had to give their son to him for his parenting time in the court order. She let him see their son for the first time in two months and they enjoyed a few hours together.

William asked himself the Five Questions:

1. ***Is the consequence proportional to the limit that I have set?***
   Yes! Going to the police to get time with my son seemed necessary because just setting the limit (for Connie to follow the court order) didn't change her behavior in over two months.
2. ***Have I considered positive consequences as well as negative consequences?***
   Yes, I offered to keep working on her car as a favor if she just left us alone and let me see our son.
3. ***Is the consequence safe?***
   Yes! The police will keep it safe.
4. ***Am I ready to enforce my consequence?***
   Yes! After two months already.
5. ***Do I need to get help in imposing my consequence?***
   Yes, and I got the police to go with me.

But there was a bit of pushback. After he had come to her house with the police to enforce the parenting schedule in the court order, Connie decided to go to court seeking a Temporary Restraining Order (TRO)—against William coming to *her house*!

At the court hearing, the judge denied Connie's TRO request. She still kept their son from going to see his father according to the court-ordered parenting plan.

What should William do? He decided to file a motion for a contempt of court orders. At the hearing, Connie claimed that she didn't have time to prepare because she was not properly served in time with the court papers. William insisted that his "Proof of Service" was in the court file and in the court computer, but he unfortunately didn't have a copy with him and the court didn't have the file at the hearing because of a shortage of staff. (Always bring extra copies if you go to court.)

But the judge said to Connie: "If you are lying to me and blocking your son's parenting time with his father, then I may have to find you in contempt of court orders at the next hearing and place you in jail for a few days. I hope that won't be necessary.

Outcome: Suddenly, Connie followed the court-ordered parenting plan. The judge re-set the hearing to keep an eye on the case.

Step 2½: EAR Statement (or Not)

Since the situation was escalated beyond their earlier amicable relationship, William decided to be firm on his limits without adding any EAR Statements because Connie had become so difficult.

However, the judge did add to his threat of jail time that he "hoped it wouldn't be necessary." This shows some empathy for Connie.

Discussion

This case shows things going from okay to worse. Apparently, the jealousy of William having his girlfriend move in was too much for Connie to bear. This happens sometimes when people get divorced but still hold out hope that they will reconcile. When the Ex has a new partner, starts living with the partner, gets married, and/or has a child with the new partner, then the reality of it really sets in. This appears to be an example of that. Connie apparently couldn't control herself, so she interfered with William in several ways: through their daughter spying, dropping by his house, and discouraging their son from spending time with him.

This situation presented William with three areas for setting limits. First, he told his daughter, who was now an adult, to move out and back with her mother. Just setting this limit was sufficient with their daughter.

Second, he gave her the positive consequence of continuing to work on Connie's car from time to time if she just stopped dropping by at his home uninvited. But she just rejected that out of hand: "I don't care!"

Third, in order to get cooperation for his parenting time with his son, friendly communication seemed to have hit a dead end. Therefore, filing for a court hearing to enforce that made sense. However, family courts are very hesitant to impose contempt of court penalties because they are a form of criminal action (since some could go to jail) and family courts are considered civil courts with lesser procedural requirements. Alternatives are to order changes in the parenting plan, like the case of Oscar in this chapter, or to order financial penalties such as a fine or "sanction" for violating the court's orders. However, if a judge really knows the case and thinks that nothing else is strong enough, putting a parent in jail for contempt of court orders is a legal option. The rare instances when this occurs are usually when a parent may be hundreds of thousands of dollars behind on child support.

DAUGHTER RESISTS SEEING DAD

Background

Lester and his former wife divorced three years ago. Their daughter, Akea, was 13 when they separated. For their parenting plan, Lester wanted to have a 50-50 equal shared custody arrangement, but his ex-wife wanted to have primary custody about 80% of the parenting time, saying that Akea felt uncomfortable at Lester's new apartment. They went to family court about the parenting schedule and the judge ordered the mother's requested schedule because of Akea's resistance.

Over the next three years Akea increasingly reduced her contact with her father. She told him she didn't want him to come to her school events and scheduled more and more time with friends during the summers. He acquiesced. Eventually, she only spent a few hours on the weekend without any overnights. On her sixteenth birthday, she sent him this handwritten letter by certified mail:

Lester, I no longer want to have a relationship with you. I believe I am old enough to make this decision. You have not respected my boundaries and you have never apologized for how you ruined my life. Now, my boundary is that you should have no further contact with me. Don't send me cards or letters, and don't try to call or text me. Also, please tell your parents not to try to contact me or send me any cards or letters or anything either.

This does not mean that I won't need financial help from you for my summer camps and planning for college. If you care about me at all you will keep supporting me that way but respect my boundary of having no further contact with you.

Lester was devastated to receive this letter. It just felt all wrong to him and that she had totally given in to her mother's anger at him for the divorce and her need to cling to their daughter as she was growing up and becoming more independent. Yet Lester questioned himself about what he had done wrong. True, he initiated the divorce but he didn't have an affair or anything. He wasn't abusive in any way. There was nothing out of the ordinary about his parenting to apologize for. In fact, he had probably let his wife push him around too much. He was always walking on eggshells around her. Maybe that's how his daughter felt now. Maybe Akea wanted to calm down her mother.

He thought about whether he should "respect" her boundary of no contact. He consulted with a therapist experienced in these types of situations when a child is "alienated" from their parent. He said he was afraid to disagree with her for fear she would hate him, as she told him once right to his face. The therapist suggested that he had the right to set limits in the relationship, as her father. She needed him to be in the adult role even though she said she wanted to reject him outright.

Step 1: Setting Limits

Here is what he decided to say in a letter and a text back to Akea:

Akea, Thanks for letting me know how you feel about your relationship with me as your father. I can understand how you might feel uncomfortable in the middle between me and your mom. However, it's not healthy for you to have no contact with your father. You need two parents. I love you and want to help you grow up into the fantastic woman I know you will be. So from time to time, I will send you cards and notes and so will my parents.

If you want financial support from me, you will need to meet with me. When it's time to apply to colleges, set up a dinner date with me and I will discuss it with you, then I'll talk with your mother about what we each will contribute. I can't support someone I don't have a relationship with. Even I have limits.

Love, Dad

Step 2: Imposing Consequences

Lester didn't hear back from Akea. But he didn't expect to. From time to time, he sent her brief notes telling her something he learned that week or did that week. He let her know he was having a happy life and enjoyed sharing it with her. He sent birthday cards and holiday cards, sometimes with a photo of where he had been and who he was with. He said he wished she would come on a trip with him someday.

She never responded, but he never expressed anger with

her about being nonresponsive. He also made copies of the letters, cards, and photos he sent her in case she didn't get them or tore them up, as she had threatened to do. The therapist had said that someday she might want to see them.

One day his ex-wife said that she needed money for Akea's summer camp and that she couldn't afford to pay anything because money was tight for her but that Lester (who was still paying her child support) made a lot of money. He said he would be happy to pay for most of the camp, but only if Akea met with him to discuss it. Soon he got a text from Akea:

Dad, you know I need money for camp. Can't you just send it to Mom?

Lester replied: *Only if you come meet with me in person to discuss it.*

Akea set up a time to meet with him. She was respectful, but brief. Lester was okay with that.

A year later, she set up a dinner meeting with him, as he had required if she wanted his financial help with college. They actually had a pleasant conversation and she agreed that she would send him updates on where she decided to apply.

Once she left her mother's home for college, their relationship thawed and became more relaxed. She even sent him texts about her successes, her frustrations, and her adventures.

How did Lester Answer the Five Questions?

1. ***Is the consequence proportional to the limit that I have set?***
   Yes. By saying he would still send notes and cards he was being a reasonable parent. It made sense that he would only provide financial support for camps and college if she met with him, as any normal parent would do.
2. ***Have I considered positive consequences as well as negative consequences?***

Yes. If she just met with him, he would give her money for camps and college. That's positive. If she didn't, then he wouldn't, which was the negative consequence.

3. ***Is the consequence safe?***
   Yes. It was just about contact and money.
4. ***Am I ready to enforce my consequence?***
   Yes. While Lester was hesitant to upset Akea, he learned that he needed to set limits, and he did.
5. ***Do I need to get help in imposing my consequence?***
   Yes. He got help from the therapist he consulted. Also, his ex-wife apparently reinforced his message to Akea, that she needed to simply meet with him in order to get financial assistance.

Step 2½: EAR Statement (or Not)

This was a case for lots of EAR Statements, even in the face of rejection. Akea was the child and Lester was the grownup. He gave her some empathy by writing that he could "understand how you might feel uncomfortable in the middle between me and your mom." He also said words that showed respect, that she would grow into "*the fantastic woman I know you will be.*" But also important was that he didn't express anger with her. It wasn't her fault that her parents got divorced and that her mother was probably sharing her anger and opinions about it with her over the years.

Discussion

This is an increasingly common situation in high-conflict divorces. About 25% of child custody disputes in today's family courts appear to have issues of a child resisting contact with a parent. In some cases, it is because of that parent's own behavior, such as child abuse, domestic violence, or intense emotions directed at the child which become overwhelming. That's called "realistic estrangement," because it is understandable that a child would want to avoid that type of behavior.

On the other hand, in other cases when there is no abuse, it is likely because the "favored" parent is badmouthing the "rejected" parent to the child or is interfering with the child's contact with that parent or is directing intense emotional reactions against the other parent so much so that the child absorbs that parent's intense emotions. That is called "parental alienation." Sometimes dad is the rejected parent and sometimes mom is the rejected parent. Some families spend years in court fighting over whether the child's resistance is mom's fault or dad's fault.

In these types of cases, it's not unusual for a child to tell one parent that they want to cut off all contact. It relieves the immediate tension for them. But that creates a big dilemma for the rejected parent, because they want to abide by their child's wishes, but they also know that it isn't normal or healthy for the child.

This case example demonstrated how this can be handled in a successful way in some cases—by setting limits and imposing consequences by sending cards and withholding money when necessary. It is interesting to note that in this case Akea called her father Lester, rather than Dad in her letter to him. That is common with children who have become alienated—they speak disrespectfully of and to that parent. However, did you notice that when she texted him later she called him "Dad," which she always used to do. His limits seem to have convinced her to treat him with more respect, because he respected himself in the relationship.

Ultimately, in many of these cases when there is no abuse history, the court may need to order blocks of time with the rejected parent and the child to overcome the negative story that the child may have heard for years from their "favored" parent. These are complex cases and parents should get knowledgeable consultation from therapists or lawyers on how to handle them.

Conclusion

Divorce situations present numerous opportunities for individuals, parents, professionals, and the courts to set limits and impose consequences. Yet most cases are resolved out of court by formal written agreements that are filed with the court. These may be negotiated with a mediator, with the help of family lawyers, or by the parties on their own. For these cases, building in consequences for failure to follow through on agreements is a good idea. Usually, they don't need to be extreme consequences, but still should be done with full legal knowledge of the risks and common solutions. Making good parenting and financial plans can be some of the most important decisions in one's life.

On the other hand, in the approximately twenty percent of divorce cases that are "high conflict," setting detailed limits and imposing detailed consequences can be the most important parts. If this is done well, it can help people stay on track and be responsible parents and Ex's. It is always recommended to consult with or retain attorneys in high-conflict cases. If things don't go well, then the courts are the normal location for getting assistance with imposing consequences for violation of the limits in court orders. However, courts are primarily designed for making decisions that people will follow automatically. Managing bad behavior and enforcing court orders are still a new area for the courts. They are slowly adapting as the need appears to be growing.

CHAPTER 7

FRIENDS

Many college students take on part-time jobs during or shortly after their studies, often working alongside classmates or close friends. These early work experiences help develop essential life skills but can also introduce new challenges. When friendships overlap with professional responsibilities, conflicts may arise around communication, accountability, and expectations—especially when both individuals are navigating their first job and learning workplace boundaries.

Separately, students living in shared dormitory settings must balance their desire for social connection with respect for neighbors' needs for quiet and study time. Conflicts commonly arise over noise and boundaries, and resolving these conflicts requires clear communication and enforcement of community standards.

While most students manage these transitions successfully, tensions can escalate when one person repeatedly crosses boundaries—whether by missing shifts and relying on a friend to cover at work, or by hosting loud gatherings that disturb dorm neighbors. These situations can be particularly difficult to navigate because personal relationships and shared living environments blur the lines of acceptable behavior.

This section presents structured examples of how emerging adults can set limits and enforce consequences in common college conflicts. One example involves friends working their first job together, addressing issues of uneven workload and accountability. Another focuses on a dorm noise complaint, illustrating how university housing staff set clear expectations and consequences to maintain community well-being. Both highlight the importance of balancing empathy, respect, and firm limits.

COLLEGE DORMMATES AND NOISE COMPLAINTS

Background

Jasmine, a 19-year-old college sophomore, lived in the university dorms alongside her friend and neighbor Priya. Known for her friendly and outgoing nature, Jasmine regularly hosted friends in her room, often playing music late into the night. However, she never considered asking Priya if she minded having guests over. This oversight led to multiple noise complaints from Priya, whose studies and sleep were disrupted by the late-night gatherings. As a result, Priya's academic performance suffered, but despite receiving informal warnings from the dorm staff, Jasmine continued her loud social activities.

After three months of unresolved complaints, the university's Residential Life Office scheduled a hearing with Jasmine to address the repeated violations of the quiet hours policy. According to university rules, quiet hours were from 10:00 p.m. to 8:00 a.m., and violations could result in disciplinary consequences, including possible removal from university housing.

Step 1: Setting Limits

At the hearing, the housing coordinator spoke directly to Jasmine:

Coordinator: "Jasmine, we've reviewed the complaint reports and informal notices. It appears you've continued playing loud music during quiet hours. We want to help you remain in your housing, but this behavior needs to stop."

Jasmine: "I understand. I didn't realize how late it had gotten some nights. I'll make sure it doesn't happen again."

Coordinator: "Let's be clear. If there's one more confirmed noise violation during quiet hours in the next 30 days, you'll be reassigned to off-campus housing. Do you understand the consequences?"

Jasmine: "Yes, I understand. It won't happen again."

The coordinator documented the conversation and followed up with an email summarizing the expectations and potential consequences.

Step 2: Imposing Consequences

Two weeks later, a resident advisor documented another violation. Jasmine hosted a small gathering with music and loud conversations past midnight on a Thursday. Priya and two other residents filed formal complaints, and security was called.

The Residential Life Office followed up with Jasmine.

Coordinator: "We had hoped you'd take the last conversation seriously. This is your third documented noise violation, and the second since our formal warning. Can you explain what happened?"

Jasmine: "Honestly, I was just trying to celebrate my friend's birthday. I didn't think it would get that loud. I guess I messed up. I didn't mean to disrespect the rules—I just lost track of time."

Coordinator: "We hear you. But this is exactly the kind of situation we warned about. Unfortunately, we're going to follow through on the consequence we outlined: you'll be reassigned to university-approved off-campus housing starting next week."

How Did the Coordinator Answer the Five Questions?

1. ***Is the consequence proportional to the limit that I have set?***
   Yes. Jasmine was warned clearly, and the result was previously communicated.
2. ***Have I considered positive consequences as well as negative consequences?***
   The coordinator offered Jasmine a chance to remain in housing and set a time window for behavior change.
3. ***Is the consequence safe?***
   Yes. Reassigning her to off-campus housing is within policy and safety protocols.
4. ***Am I ready to enforce my consequence?***
   Yes. Housing has procedures in place to process the reassignment immediately.
5. ***Do I need to get help in imposing my consequence?***
   No. The Coordinator and the Residential Life Office has the authority to carry this out independently. However, if you think in terms of Priya, she did need the help of the Residential Life Office to enforce this consequence, so her answer would be: Yes.

Step 2½: EAR Statement (or Not)

Before ending the meeting, the coordinator offered an EAR Statement:

Coordinator: "I know this may feel like a big consequence, and I appreciate that you're taking responsibility. I also recognize that you care about your friends and building community. But your neighbors have a right to quiet and rest, and we've reached a point where words are no longer enough. We still want you to succeed here, and we're here to support your transition. If you need help finding new housing or adjusting to the change, please reach out."

Discussion

This is a clear example of setting limits and enforcing consequences in a structured student conduct setting. The student was given a fair chance to correct her behavior, and the consequence—while difficult—was directly related to the rule violated. This fairness is a cornerstone of our disciplinary process, ensuring that all students are treated equitably.

The EAR Statement helped balance enforcement with empathy. Jasmine might be more mindful in future shared living environments, and she'll likely reflect on how community living requires respect for others' needs. Consequences, when followed through consistently, often lead to growth—especially for emerging adults navigating independence. This incident underscores the importance of community respect, a core value in our shared living spaces. It also teaches Jasmine a life lesson that may steer her in a more positive direction throughout her adulthood.

FRIENDS AT FIRST JOB – BROKEN WORK AGREEMENT

Background

Trina and Dani were close friends throughout college. After graduating, they both secured positions as research assistants at a local nonprofit focused on environmental policy. This was their first professional job, and they were excited to work together. Early on, they informally agreed to "split tasks" for their shared assignments—taking turns summarizing reports, formatting presentations, and managing emails from their project supervisors. It felt like teamwork, and they even joked that they made a great "two-for-one" hire.

However, over time, Dani began to fall behind. She missed deadlines, frequently asked Trina to cover for her "just this once," and started arriving late to meetings. When supervisors asked questions, Trina covered for her at first. Eventually, Trina realized that she was doing nearly all the shared work while Dani continued to receive equal credit. This imbalance began to affect Trina's reputation and mental health. She didn't want to jeopardize their friendship, but she also didn't want to lose credibility at her first job. Seeking advice, Trina called her older cousin, who worked in HR. Her cousin said, "Friendship or not, you're both employees now. You don't owe her silence. Try setting a limit and giving her a chance to change before involving anyone else. But if she continues to exploit your silence, you'll need to escalate the situation. You're not the backup."

Step 1: Setting Limits

The next day, Trina pulled Dani aside after lunch.

Trina: "Hey, I wanted to talk to you about our projects. I've noticed I've been doing the bulk of our shared assignments lately—like the last two reports and the presentation slide deck. I know things get busy, but I can't keep doing more than my share, especially since we both get credit."

Dani seemed a little surprised but didn't interrupt.

Trina: "I value our friendship, and this is why I pulled you aside rather than sharing my concerns as a problem with the team. From now on, let's split tasks formally: I'll handle the first half of each research section, and you'll do the second. Ok? If something comes up, just let me know—but I won't be stepping in last-minute anymore. If this happens again, I have to let our supervisor know."

Dani said she understood and appreciated Trina coming to her directly.

Step 2: Imposing Consequences

Unfortunately, two weeks later, Dani flaked again. She promised to finish her half of the monthly report, but when Trina checked the shared document the night before the deadline, it was nearly blank. Trina didn't edit it this time. Instead, she emailed their supervisor:

"Hi Alexis, I wanted to flag that our team's monthly report is only partially complete. I finished my half, but Dani's section wasn't submitted as planned. I wanted to be transparent since the deadline is tomorrow."

The next morning, their supervisor met with both of them. Dani looked uncomfortable but didn't argue. Supervisor: "Moving forward, I'll be assigning tasks individually. That way, responsibility is clear. Trina, thank you for your communication. Dani, I expect your next task will be submitted on time—solo." Dani's professional image took a hit. Trina didn't feel good about it, but she felt relieved that she warned Dani of the consequences and went through with it.

How Did Trina Answer the Five Questions?

1. ***Is the consequence proportional to the limit that I have set?***
   Yes. She first set a verbal limit, and only after a repeated pattern did she inform their supervisor.
2. ***Have I considered positive consequences as well as negative consequences?***
   Yes. Dani had a chance to fix things privately, and the supervisor didn't punish her—just removed shared credit.
3. ***Is the consequence safe?***
   Yes. Trina didn't raise her voice or shame Dani—she simply protected her credibility.
4. ***Am I ready to enforce my consequence?***
   Yes. Trina followed through by refusing to cover for Dani and informing the supervisor when the pattern repeated.

5. ***Do I need to get help in imposing my consequence?***
   Yes. The supervisor played a role in making consequences clear and adjusting future workflows.

Various outcomes in situations like this depend on Dani's personality:

A. Accountable but overwhelmed Dani: Dani came to Trina a few days later and said, "You were right—I've been overwhelmed and relied on you too much. I'll manage my tasks going forward." Their friendship slowly recovered, and Dani became more reliable.

B. Embarrassed but resentful Dani: Dani never admitted fault, but she stopped asking Trina for help. She kept her distance at work, and their friendship faded. Still, Trina's reputation at work improved, and she gained confidence in handling workplace conflict.

C. High-conflict Dani: Dani told coworkers Trina "ratted her out," and even suggested Trina was trying to sabotage her. But Trina had the documentation to back up her work. Their supervisor eventually gave Dani a warning for unprofessional behavior.

Step 2½: EAR Statement (or Not)

In this case, Trina included some EAR elements in her first conversation: Empathy: "I know things get busy." Attention: "If something comes up, let me know. I'll pay attention." Respect: "I wanted to talk to you first before this becomes a problem." She made her limit clear without turning it into a personal attack. Her calm tone helped preserve dignity and left the door open for change.

Discussion

This is a common situation for young professionals—blurring the line between friendship and professional expectations. Trina learned an essential workplace skill: setting respectful boundaries without waiting for a crisis. She also learned that protecting your reputation doesn't mean burning bridges. Through clear communication and consistent follow-through, she earned respect from her supervisor while giving Dani a fair chance to improve. With clear communication and follow-through, she earned respect from her supervisor and gave Dani a fair chance to improve. Friendships can survive growing pains—but only when both people are willing to grow.

Conclusion

In this chapter we focused on friendships in college and new jobs. However, the same issues arise for all age groups in friendships, especially when living together or working close together. A lot of how these situations go depends on whether one or both people have a high-conflict personality or tendencies in that direction. By thinking in terms of setting limits and imposing consequences right from the start of living or working together, it often is possible to get a friendship back on track by speaking up sooner rather than later. It is common to assume that the other person shares the same standards and habits, when in fact they might be able to adapt before things become too tense if they can just talk about it. On the other hand, when a high-conflict person is involved, things often just get worse unless limits are set and consequences are imposed sooner rather than later. Initial friendship should not be a basis for tolerating a bad situation.

CHAPTER 8

COMMUNITY

Conflicts within communities, whether in apartment complexes or residential neighborhoods, can disrupt harmony and escalate into significant disputes if left unaddressed. These disagreements often stem from misunderstandings, differences in lifestyles, or the failure to establish clear communication between residents. When tensions rise, minor inconveniences can quickly snowball into resentment, leading to personal attacks, retaliatory actions, and even legal disputes.

In this series of case studies, we examine real-life conflicts that have emerged in communal living spaces and explore strategies for resolution. From rebuilding neighborly relations to addressing persistent noise disturbances, each scenario highlights the importance of setting boundaries, enforcing consequences, and utilizing effective communication techniques such as EAR Statements (Empathy, Attention, Respect). By understanding the root causes of these conflicts and applying structured resolution methods, individuals can foster a more peaceful and cooperative living environment.

Through these examples, we will explore how conflict resolution techniques—such as mediation, setting clear behavioral expectations, and establishing accountability—can de-escalate tensions and promote a respectful coexistence among neighbors. These case studies serve as a guide for individuals facing similar disputes, offering insight into how proactive communication and conflict resolution strategies can prevent minor disagreements from evolving into full-blown crises.

By learning from these real-world examples, communities can work towards fostering a culture of mutual respect, understanding, and cooperation, ensuring that shared living spaces remain places of comfort rather than contention.

NEIGHBOR HOSTILITY IN APARTMENT COMPLEX

Background

Tensions between two neighboring families in an apartment complex had been building for months. Initially, disagreements were minor: disputes over noise levels, parking spots, and shared spaces. However, these minor conflicts escalated, leading to resentment between the two households. Eventually, the hostility extended beyond the adults and began affecting their children, who started bullying one another at school and within the apartment complex.

One evening, the situation reached a breaking point. During a heated exchange, one family made an insulting remark about the other's way of living, implying that they did not respect the shared space and that their cultural background was known to be uneducated and stupid overall.

Neighbor 1: "You people always act like you own this place! You never think about how your actions affect the rest of us."

Neighbor 2: "Excuse me? We've been nothing but respectful. If anyone is causing problems, it's your kids, always excuses and picking fights."

Neighbor 1: "Maybe if you taught them some manners,

they wouldn't be such a nuisance!"

Neighbor 2: "Oh, now you're blaming us for everything? You're the ones always stirring up drama!"

Feeling provoked, the father from the family of Neighbor 2 lost his temper and retaliated by keying the back of Neighbor 1's car, leaving a deep scratch across the surface.

Step 1. Setting Limits

Neighbor 1 decided to take legal action and brought the matter to small claims court. The judge sent both families to mediation to resolve it. If there was no luck in mediation, then they would come back for the hearing before the judge.

In mediation they discussed setting limits on future actions to prevent further escalation. Both families agreed to respect the shared spaces within the apartment complex, to be mindful of noise levels, parking spaces, and use of common areas without leaving personal items behind. Furthermore, both families committed to resolving conflicts calmly and respectfully without resorting to insults or physical retaliation.

If disagreements arise, they agreed that they must be addressed through open and respectful communication, and if necessary, mediation should be sought before taking further action. The children's behavior was equally important, and both families agreed to tell their children the importance of respecting one another. Bullying or aggressive behavior, whether in the apartment complex or at school, would not be tolerated and would be addressed with appropriate action, including involvement from school authorities if necessary.

Additionally, they agreed that insulting remarks or personal attacks, especially those related to cultural background or lifestyle, must be avoided at all costs. Both families agreed that any personal insults would cause an immediate apology, and future communications will be conducted with respect. Lastly, destructive behavior, such as damaging property or engaging in physical altercations, would have serious consequences. Any property damage would cause legal action, and the responsible party will be held financially accountable. These limits aim to ensure that both families can coexist peacefully, with a clear understanding of acceptable behaviors and the consequences for violating them.

Step 2: Impose Consequences

This is one of those cases in which the damage was done before anyone could set limits against having a car "keyed." Yet that is property damage which is already illegal under the law. This is not unusual, in that consequences often need to be imposed without a prior setting limits discussion because the action is already against the law. Therefore, while setting other limits was discussed in mediation, the consequence for the damage still needed to be addressed.

Luckily, both families reached a settlement. The father responsible for the damage agreed to pay for a complete repainting of the car, as estimated by a professional mechanic, with payments over the next 6 months. If any problems occurred with the payment plan, then they agreed that they would come back to mediation first.

How Did Neighbor 1 Answer the Five Questions?

1. ***Is the consequence proportional to the limit that I have set?***
   Yes. Agreeing to have the car repainted at Neighbor 2's expense is directly proportional as Neighbor 2 caused the expense. This is more proportional than if Neighbor 1 had sought criminal action against Neighbor 2.
2. ***Have I considered positive consequences as well as negative consequences?***
   Yes. Agreeing to monthly payments was a positive

consequence that Neighbor 1 accepted (so long as payments are made). Demanding immediate payment would have been a purely negative consequence, which Neighbor 1 could have asked for, but probably would have gotten less cooperation and escalated tensions unnecessarily.

3. ***Is the consequence safe?***
   Yes.
4. ***Am I ready to enforce my consequence?***
   Yes. Neighbor 1 already took this case to Small Claims Court and will easily do it again if necessary.
5. ***Do I need to get help in imposing my consequence?***
   Possibly. If payments aren't made, then Neighbor 1 will proceed back to court.

Step 2½: EAR Statement (or Not)

During the mediation the mediator gave the parties several EAR Statements throughout the process. Perhaps because of this, Neighbor 2 was able to say the following to Neighbor 1: "I understand that you were upset about your car being damaged, and I take full responsibility for what I did. I regret my actions and realize I let my anger get the best of me. I want to make things right, so I agreed to pay for the repair. Moving forward, I want us to have a more peaceful relationship for our families. I hope we can respect each other's space and communicate better."

Neighbor 1 thanked Neighbor 2 and agreed with the goal of more peaceful future contact.

This agreement was presented to the Small Claims Court judge, who happily approved it. The judge also complimented the parties on reaching an agreement, saying that he had a lot of respect for them and that they were role models for solving neighbor problems.

Having a judge give an EAR Statement—in this case emphasizing Respect—can go a long way to future peace between the neighbors. Ongoing relationships like this can benefit a lot when dispute resolvers such as mediators and judges give them a lot of empathy, attention, and/or respect. This may make the difference between future problems or stronger efforts to get along.

Discussion

This case gave us an example of imposing a consequence when a limit already existed under the law. Rather than pursuing a criminal case against Neighbor 2, Neighbor 1 took the case to Small Claims Court which can impose financial consequences up to a certain amount, such as $12,000 maximum in some locations. Since it will cost less than that to paint the car, this is a proportional consequence. If Neighbor 1 had sought criminal charges against Neighbor 2, it would have been disproportional and escalated tensions so high that they probably would not be able to live in the same complex anymore.

This case also demonstrated the benefit of having a dispute go to mediation before having the case heard in court. A majority of cases brought to mediation do reach agreements (60-80 percent), which saves the courts and the parties a lot of money. Mediation has grown rapidly over the past forty years and people can use it in almost any dispute, whether referred by the court or totally voluntary from the start. With ongoing relationships, like parents after a divorce, neighbors in conflict, and business disputes, mediation can help resolve a problem without damaging the good will that may have existed before. When judges approve mediation agreements with an EAR Statement, it often gives a boost to the parties to maintain a positive relationship in the future.

For a mediator, giving both parties EAR Statements can be highly beneficial, especially when emotions are heightened and tensions need to be de-escalated. EAR Statements allow individuals to feel empathy, demonstrate understanding of the other person's feelings, and show respect for their perspective. In this case, the responsible father used an EAR Statement to acknowledge the damage caused, express regret for his actions, and commit to making amends.

This case also involved insulting remarks which targeted cultural backgrounds and parenting styles, ignited anger, further pushing both families away from resolving the conflict peacefully. In this context, establishing clear limits and consequences for disruptive behavior in mediation was essential to prevent further escalation and to foster a cooperative, respectful living environment. By addressing these behavioral problems in a positive, future-oriented way, the families can rebuild their relationship and avoid future destructive actions.

TENANT PARKING SPACE DISPUTE

Background

In an apartment complex, a young property manager who also was a tenant faced ongoing issues with a tenant who repeatedly violated property rules. The tenant had been parking two cars side-by-side in a single parking spot, obstructing part of the driveway. Despite the property manager's explanation that only one parking space per unit was allowed, the tenant continued to park one of his cars in other residents' designated spots.

Additionally, the tenant had not adhered to the required rent increase under state law, continuing to pay the previous year's rate. He also left Amazon boxes in the walkway, obstructing the entrance and creating a safety hazard.

Step 1: Setting Limits

The property manager was young and appreciated the reduced rate for her apartment since she was performing the duties of the property manager. She got up her nerve and went to confront the older male tenant—again.

Property Manager: "I've noticed you're still parking two cars in one spot. You're only allowed one parking space per unit, as per the lease agreement. You need to move your second vehicle."

Tenant: "Are you just repeating yourself? I heard you the first time."

Property Manager: "I understand, but I'm reminding you again because it still violates the rules. You need to move the second car immediately. It's blocking other people's spots and the driveway."

Tenant: "I don't see the problem. It's not that big of a deal."

Property Manager: "It is a problem because it takes up someone else's parking spot and creates a driving hazard. You are also not paying the rent increase as required by state law. You must pay the updated rent rate, or you'll violate your lease."

Tenant: "I'm paying what I've always paid. I'm not paying more."

Property Manager: "Unfortunately, that's not an option. You must pay the increased rent. Also, you've been leaving Amazon boxes in the walkway, blocking the entrance. This is a safety issue and needs to be addressed immediately; please clear the walkway by removing your empty boxes."

Tenant: "I don't care about the boxes. I'll move them when I get to it."

Limits may not work effectively in this case due to the tenant's consistent defiance and dismissiveness toward authority. The tenant has already shown a pattern of ignoring the rules. The tenant's minimization of safety concerns, such as leaving Amazon boxes in the walkway and stating he doesn't care, further indicates that limits may not have the desired impact.

Step 2: Imposing Consequences

There are many rules and required procedures for landlords and tenants throughout the country. The young property manager will need to learn those and follow them. Since they are so clear-cut, all she needs is the confidence to implement them.

The consequences for non-compliance with the property rules should be carried out in stages. First, the tenant must be given a formal ***written reminder*** regarding the parking rules, the required rent increase, and the safety concerns, including the Amazon boxes blocking the walkway. This reminder must set clear compliance deadlines. The young property manager did that and hand delivered it to the tenant.

But the tenant continued to disregard the rules. In that case, the second offense caused a ***formal warning and rent adjustment notification***, with a final reminder that should the tenant still fail to comply, the third offense will cause the initiation of ***lease violation procedures***, which may include legal action to recover unpaid rent or damages, and ***eviction proceedings***.

Will the manager enforce these consequences? Will the tenant comply?

How Did the Property Manager Answer the Five Questions?

1. ***Is the consequence proportional to the limit that I have set?***
   Yes. Non-compliance with parking rules, rent requirements and safety rules to not block the entrance are important and proportional after many warnings.

2. ***Have I considered positive consequences as well as negative consequences?***
   Yes. The manager gave the tenant more warnings and chances than necessary.
3. ***Is the consequence safe?***
   Yes. There is no indication that the tenant will be dangerous to her personally and the consequences may become serious but not dangerous for the tenant.
4. ***Am I ready to enforce my consequence?***
   Yes. The young property manager was very frustrated with this tenant, who was disrespectful toward her as well as having multiple violations. Time for action.
5. ***Do I need to get help in imposing my consequence?***
   Yes. She spoke to the owner who gave her the required formal paperwork to notify the tenant of the beginning of eviction proceedings and legal action to recover the unpaid rent.

Step 2½: EAR Statement (or Not)

Since this was an ongoing relationship for the property manager and the tenant, she had decided to try some empathy at the start of setting limits: "I understand that you may feel the parking issue isn't a big deal, but these rules are in place to ensure everyone has fair access to the resources they're entitled to. I respect your right to disagree, but these rules are set to maintain order and safety within the complex."

However, by the second and third violations and notices, it was clear to her that EAR was not helping and that she was just being manipulated and dismissed. After she gave him the third notice, which included the start of the eviction process, he abruptly moved out. He left a mess and obviously didn't care.

Discussion

This tenant was apparently a high-conflict person with extreme behavior that 90% of people would never exhibit. The owner would need to deal with him through the legal process. The young property manager had done all she could do, with empathy and clear limits. The consequences were properly imposed following all the rules and procedures.

The age and gender difference did not seem to make a difference in this case. It was the tenant's personality to act as he did and there was nothing obvious that the property manager could have done differently. The owner was a man and the tenant's behavior toward him was ultimately dismissive and non-compliant.

This case shows the benefit of having established rules, laws, and procedures for setting limits and imposing consequences. The property manager just had to build up the courage to implement them. Ironically, the tenant's dismissive attitude helped build her resolve.

Would mediation have helped in this case? While that was not used, given his ultimate action of leaving abruptly, it appears that it would not have made a difference.

The next case shows the use of mediation with a similarly resistant homeowner.

HIGH-CONFLICT HOMEOWNER

Background

Ten years ago, Manny bought a house in a pleasant neighborhood at the end of a cul-de-sac in a small mid-west city. He began to tear it down to build his dream home. He showed the neighbors how beautiful the new home would look, based on a well-worn magazine photograph. He had a recent and sizable inheritance to work with and he assured everyone it would be done within six months.

Before he was finished tearing down the old house he moved in with his new girlfriend, and stopped working on his new house. Months went by without him being seen. Yet the rubble, boards, nails and broken glass remained on the site of his old house. One day, two of the neighbor children playing in the abandoned debris cut themselves on broken window glass. The neighbors were outraged and began meeting to decide what to do.

Step 1: Setting Limits

The neighbors decided to take legal action. The site of the house was now an "attractive nuisance" to their children. The neighbors went to town council and were told to try mediation first.

Mediation: Six of the neighbors attended the mediation, as well as Manny. He was extremely apologetic. "I got sidetracked with my business, which had a downturn. After I get the money together, I'm going to start right up again finishing the house. I'm really sorry for the delays. They were just unavoidable. Trust me; I'll take care of it right away."

"But we thought you had enough money to do the project from the start," said Fred, one of the neighbors, with some degree of irritation. "Didn't you have an inheritance?"

"Well, yeah," Manny admitted. Then he was all smiles again. "I had to use it to get my business through the downturn. I just need another $10,000 to get it finished. I'll start again after I raise the money. I always keep my promises."

"But the job site is dangerous now, especially to the children," replied Fred. "You need to start working again right now."

"Give him a break, Fred," said Carrie, another friendly neighbor. "Can't you see that he's struggling to handle his business? Maybe we can help him put up a high fence to protect the children."

"Oh, a fence is a great idea. Don't worry, I can take care of that myself," Manny said. "I'll put one up this week. I'm a man of my word, I assure you."

Afterward, Fred said to Carrie: "I don't trust him for a minute. He told everyone he would do it in six months, and that was a year ago. Besides, I get a cold feeling when I'm around him."

"But you know how many delays there can be in construction," Carrie countered in defense of Manny. "I'm sure he'll get a fence up this week."

Two weeks later, Carrie finally tracked down Manny's phone number. He had given them a cell phone number at the meeting, but it was no longer in service. She was furious.

"Get that fence up and start working, Manny," she exclaimed. "I want that project done within six months!"

"Sure, sure," Manny replied. "Calm down. I just got some more money in, so I'll get started this weekend. Business problems just came up again that I had no control over. Even you said to give me a break. Thanks so much for your understanding. I'm a businessman and I know how important it is to keep good relations going. You've really been wonderful to support me on this. Not everyone has been so understanding. Thanks again."

Carrie said later that Manny had completely reassured her, and that she believed in him again. He made her feel so good — that she was being so helpful to someone having business problems.

Finally, the fence went up and the rest of the house was cleared away. Then there was no sign of Manny for **another year**—except for the ugly seven-foot construction fence around the empty lot. The neighbors decided it was time to take stronger action. They did some research and found out that Manny was reporting to the city that the empty lot was his principal place of residence. They found out that he was living with his girlfriend on the other side of town. They finally found out his new phone number, a number that kept changing for some reason. But they couldn't find any record of a business in his name.

Step 2: Imposing Consequences

They finally decided to sue him. Ten neighbors were now furious about his inaction and his constant lying about working on the house. They decided to sue him in small claims court, for a maximum of $5,000 each. A $50,000 judgment would move him to action, they figured, and besides, they wouldn't need a lawyer in small claims court, so it wouldn't cost them too much.

At court they were all ready with their papers and photos and other exhibits. When the small claims commissioner started the hearing, Manny announced that he thought he had a solution that he wanted to discuss with the neighbors. The commissioner said: "That's wonderful. I always prefer a good settlement to a court-imposed decision."

Manny told them he would sell the lot, someone else could build, and the problem would be solved. Since the neighbors weren't sure if they would ever see their $50,000 even if they won, they believed that this solution would get rid of Manny, so they agreed. They drew up a contract in which Manny agreed he would immediately sell the house. If his name was still on title after ninety days, then he agreed that they could enter a judgment against him in the full amount of $50,000.

How Did the Neighbors Answer the Five Questions?

1. ***Is the consequence proportional to the limit that was set?***
   Yes. Manny would make the money from selling his house. If he failed to perform, then the $50,000 penalty was appropriate.
2. ***Have I considered positive consequences as well as negative consequences?***

Yes. They accepted Manny's solution of him selling his house, which was a positive consequence.

3. ***Is the consequence safe?***
   Yes.
4. ***Were they ready to enforce their consequence?***
   Yes. They had a binding contract that would pay them $50,000 if he failed to sell.
5. ***Do I need to get help in imposing my consequence?***
   Yes. They realized that they needed to work together. They were very motivated.

Outcome: Over the next three months, no For Sale signs went up and no listings could be found in any real estate office. After ninety days they discovered that his name had been removed from the title and that a woman now owned the empty lot. It was his girlfriend. So he manipulated them again, and they could not collect the penalty.

It was **two more years** before he actually sold the house. A total of three and a half years passed from the time that Manny started tearing down the old house until the new owner completed the new house and tore down the ugly fence.

Step 2½: EAR Statement (or Not)

During the mediation, Carrie gave Manny some empathy, saying: "Give him a break. Can't you see he's struggling to handle his business." However, that didn't last long. He had conned them all, including Carrie. No more EAR Statements for Manny. Instead, they focused on trying to set firm limits and impose consequences.

Discussion

Manny is a good example of someone with high-conflict personality traits. He was charming and effectively manipulated Carrie several times. Fred had him figured out, down to the "cold feeling" that people sometimes get around someone like this, because it seemed that Manny didn't have any real empathy and don't care if he hurt them or their children.

Manny demonstrated the classic characteristics of a high-conflict person who lies a lot and switches stories to fit the moment. There was no evidence that he ever received an inheritance. He controlled situations through fast-talking and diverting attention from his behavior with new promises and excuses. He had a history of bad deals falling all around him, including his (probably) non-existent business. To continue dominating the situation he played at the edge of the rules, such as transferring the title to his girlfriend. Some high-conflict people seem to enjoy dominating others. When they are confronted, they appear to relish spinning a new con to get out of the old one. With charm and a series of manipulations, they often succeed—for a while.

It's hard to know whether the neighbors actually made a difference, or Manny did exactly what he was going to do anyway. We'll never know. However, the approach the neighbors used to set limits and impose consequences (jointly going to Small Claims Court) have probably worked for some people somewhere and are good to know they exist as an option.

[This example first appeared in Bill's book *High Conflict People in Legal Disputes* (2006). It is analyzed here because it is an unusual real-life example of homeowners banding together to set limits and impose consequences.]

TEEN GANG BEHAVIOR

Background

This tragic example demonstrates what can happen when a community at large does little to rein in high-conflict behavior—until they have to. The following information comes from an article by Rachel Monroe in *The New Yorker* magazine, July 2024.

In a rapidly growing suburban community, numerous high school boys and girls became used to teasing and drinking and bullying and fighting with each other and picking on other teens in the community, especially on the weekend. They were known as the Gilbert Goons in recent years and a similar group of wild teenagers in the same community in the 1990s was called the Devil Dogs. Both groups tended to have "high-school athletes from privileged families who liked to beat up strangers, and who filmed their fights" on videocassettes in the 1990s and on their cell phones in the 2000s. The Goons also included "some older guys: recent grads, dropouts, older brothers."

On a Saturday evening in October 2023, an open invite to a Halloween party included several of the older Goons and Preston Lord, a sophomore, and his friends. At one point, Lord and his friends left the party and walked down the street. But a group of older boys followed them. They looked like football players. They taunted the younger kids, who started to run. The older guys caught up and knocked down Lord and started kicking, beating, and "getting on him and going at it" according to witnesses.

Preston Lord never regained consciousness and died two days later.

Step 1: Setting Limits

Investigations revealed that there was a long history of tolerance in the community for this wild teenage gang-type of behavior. Younger teens at parties had been surrounded and punched and beaten unconscious. There were at least four incidents in five weeks involving brass knuckles. The self-described Goons had been "wreaking havoc" for over a year in Gilbert and surrounding communities, "with few consequences."

"The Goons had expensive vehicles and no curfews and longish hair that hung in their faces. They liked car surfing—riding on outsides of moving vehicles—and hanging out in the parking lot between the In-N-Out and the Walmart, where the boys got in fights and the girls stood around, watching them fight."

The girls engaged in bad behavior as well. Two parents of one girl said they saw her change during her sophomore year in high school when she began dating one of the boys who was later involved in the deadly attack. They found out that she had been supplying another girl with cocaine. They attempted to set limits by having a meeting with her and the school administration.

"I thought the minute we sit her down with an authority, that's going to scare her. And it didn't." The school resource officer also was intimidated by the teen-agers, including their vaping and drug use. "Well, there's two thousand of them and there's four of us. What do you want us to do?"

Also making it hard to set limits was the fact that the school system allowed students to go to any school in the district. "The troublemakers can switch schools really easily. Or kids switch schools because of bullying, or because they just don't like the kids there."

Perhaps the main reason the community didn't set limits on this behavior was that it was an upscale community with an image to maintain. Apparently, each beating was hushed up to the extent that the police said they never heard of "Gilbert Goons" until after Preston Lord's death.

But this is a situation like the Neighbor 1 at the beginning of this chapter in which the neighbor violated the law and didn't specifically need to be verbally told in advance not to scratch the other neighbor's car. The law already existed; the limits were already set—assault and battery are crimes. The question and the main problem were the lack of consequences prior to Preston Lord's death.

Step 2: Imposing Consequences

Immediately after the killing, those teens involved did what they usually did: they texted each other about it even saying "I hit him pretty hard" and commenting on who else did as well. Then they realized they needed to cover up who did it and told each other to delete their videos. But it didn't take long to determine who was involved.

Seven teens were arrested and charged with Lord's murder. In the fall of 2024 and the spring of 2025, they were given sentences of up to 17 years in prison.

How Did the Judge Seem to Answer the Five Questions?

1. ***Is the consequence proportional to the limit that the law has set?***
   Yes. The defendants were charged as adults even though they were mostly 17. There are sentencing guidelines and the judge(s) carefully weighed them.
2. ***Have I considered positive consequences as well as negative consequences?***
   Yes. In the case of one of the defendants the judge gave some of the sentence as probation (after 12 years), which creates a positive consequence for good behavior (and negative if he makes further violations).
3. ***Is the consequence safe?***
   Yes. They will be in prison. They are strong young men.
4. ***Am I ready to enforce my consequences?***
   Yes. The judge had no hesitation in sentencing the young men.
5. ***Do I need to get help in imposing my consequence?***
   Yes. The prison system will carry it out. The crimes involved were mostly felonies and the publicity and

confessions made it clear that prison sentences would be necessary. It's just too bad that this came too late to prevent Preston Lord's murder.

Step 2½: EAR Statement (or Not)

The judge in one of the sentencing hearings noted that the defendant had ignored several wake-up calls from prior incidents of violence. But he also added that there would be services available for his alcohol and impulsive behavior problems. That may be a slight amount of empathy. Mostly, sentencing for such a public crime often requires more sternness than empathy, so that the public is reassured that justice has been done and so that others will make more of an effort to follow the law.

Discussion

This is a tragic case and all of the teens involved had their lives ruined. It is a powerful example of how society and communities need to set limits and impose consequences for violent behavior and other extremes *much sooner rather than later.* Adolescence is the best time to learn the hard way with strong consequences, so that setting limits and imposing consequences is less necessary when they become adults.

Conclusion

This chapter showed informal, formal, creative, and legal ways of setting limits and imposing consequences (or trying to impose consequences or needing to impose consequences) on neighbors. This is also an area where mediation is often used to settle these disputes because of the ongoing nature of neighbor relationships. In some cases, EAR Statements seemed important and in others they were pointless. Overall, neighborhoods are one of the most common areas for needing to set limits and impose consequences, for the sake of peaceful communities and satisfying personal lives. In most cases, setting limits is sufficient to help people get along, but as demonstrated, when high-conflict personalities are involved imposing consequences becomes very important. This is especially true with adolescents in the community who are headed in an antisocial direction. Sooner is better than later when it comes to imposing consequences, so that they can still learn before anyone gets seriously hurt and their own lives are ruined.

CHAPTER 9

SCHOOLS

This chapter presents educational struggles focused on students and setting limits—a student silenced, a friend trapped, a student leader challenged. The focus will be on identifying problematic behavior, understanding the limitations of merely setting boundaries, and emphasizing that sometimes they must be accompanied by appropriate consequences to ensure accountability and lasting change. Furthermore, in most school cases EAR Statements (empathy, attention and respect) can serve as a powerful tool for de-escalation and resolution, turning conflict into an opportunity for growth when applied strategically.

STUDENT-TEACHER CONFLICT

Background

Amelia is a dedicated student in her French class. She takes great pride in her name, Amelia, which holds personal and cultural significance as it was given in honor of a family member she reveres. However, her professor, Professor Harris, consistently mispronounces her name, calling her "Emily." Initially, Amelia believed the mistake was innocent, but when the professor continued to call her "Emily" despite repeated corrections, it became clear that her identity was not being respected. The professor also began to exaggerate the pronunciation of her name in a mocking tone, making comments like, "French names are already complicated enough; let's keep things simple." This behavior, which initially seemed minor, escalated to the point where Amelia's name appeared incorrectly on graded assignments, and the professor dismissed her requests to be addressed correctly. Amelia decided to confront the issue head-on.

Step 1: Setting Limits

PROFESSOR HARRIS: "Emily, what do you think about this sentence structure?"

AMELIA: "Actually, my name is Amelia."

PROF HARRIS: (laughs lightly) "Oh, I know, but Emily is so much easier to say. And they look similar, don't they?"

AMELIA: (calm but firm) "But it's not my name. Amelia is important to me."

PROF HARRIS: (waves hand dismissively) "Oh, come on, it's just a small change. No need to be so serious."

AMELIA: (more insistent) "I'd really appreciate it if you used my actual name."

PROF HARRIS: (sighs, shaking head) "Alright, alright. But if I slip up, don't take it personally." (Grins as if it's a joke)

The next class, Professor Harris once again calls her "Emily," despite the prior conversation. Professor Harris's persistent misnaming of Amelia, despite her repeated corrections, reflects a disregard for her personal identity. His mocking pronunciation of her name and dismissive comments, such as "It's just a name," further invalidate Amelia's feelings and the significance of her name. The professor's behavior creates a hostile environment where Amelia is publicly embarrassed and her identity is diminished. This institutional disrespect is exemplified when

Amelia's name is written incorrectly on graded assignments, showcasing a lack of regard for her identity within the academic setting. The power imbalance between the professor and Amelia makes it challenging for her to assert herself without risking further isolation.

Step 2: Imposing Consequences

To prevent any further public embarrassment, Amelia decides to ask the professor for a private meeting.

AMELIA: "I have something I want to say to you. Please, just listen until I'm done."

PROF HARRIS: "All right! Have a seat. I'm all ears."

AMELIA: "My name is integral to my identity. Continued mispronunciations are not acceptable. Mocking or exaggerated pronunciations are disrespectful, as my name is a significant part of my cultural and personal identity. Please understand that the invalidation of my feelings is not a trivial matter to me and dismissing my concerns is unacceptable. Also, my name needs to be reflected correctly on all academic materials, including graded assignments. I expect to be treated with the same respect as any other student. If my concerns are not taken seriously, I will escalate this matter to the Department Chair, and also to the Student Affairs Office if necessary. I hope I won't need to do that. I mostly enjoy your class with this one exception. Any questions?"

PROF HARRIS: "No. I'm disappointed that you took this so seriously, but I will stop. Are you done?"

AMELIA: "Yes. Thank you!"

How Did Amelia Answer the Five Questions?

1. ***Is the consequence proportional to the limit I have set?***
   Yes. Threatening to go to the Department Chair was proportionate for a professor's behavior—not too big,

not too small. This is much better than going to the media or bad-mouthing the professor online.

2. ***Have I considered positive consequences as well as negative consequences?***
   Yes. If he follows her limit she won't need to go to the Department Chair.
3. ***Is the consequence safe?***
   Yes. There is no indication that talking to the Department Chair would risk danger from Professor Harris.
4. ***Am I ready to enforce my consequences?***
   Yes. She decided she would impose her consequence since she already had imposed her first consequence of a private meeting with Professor Harris.
5. ***Do I need to get help in imposing my consequence?***
   Yes. She will go to the Department Chair for help, if necessary, as she explained. She will probably practice with a classmate before doing that.

Step 2½: EAR Statement (or Not)

Amelia knew that she needed to find a way to get along with her professor despite this problem, so she added "I mostly enjoy your class with this one exception" as a very brief statement of respect for his teaching. It may have helped.

In response, Professor Harris didn't give Amelia an EAR Statement, but he also said he would stop. That's what she really hoped to hear.

Discussion

In this case, Amelia imposes a small consequence by meeting with Professor Harris because he did not follow the limits she set each time he mispronounced her name. He didn't need to know that this would be her consequence, she just needed to do it.

However, during the meeting she made it clear that she would escalate the matter to the Department Chair and the Student Affairs Office, if necessary. That likely consequence appears to have gotten his attention and he committed himself to following her limits. Without this threatened consequence he might have simply continued to bother Amelia about her name.

In many cases, such a threatened consequence is sufficient, especially in an educational institution that is supposed to value students and treat them with respect. In today's world, most educational organizations understand that students are also consumers and that their needs should be valued. If Professor Harris does continue misusing her name, it is clear what she will do. Whether the Department Chair and Student Affairs Office take any action is unclear. If not, in some Universities there is an Ombudsman Office which is designed to assist with such matters or possibly Human Resources could help. We know that Amelia will take action because she feels strongly enough about this issue and the Professor's behavior is clearly out of line. Perhaps someone with a high-conflict personality.

CLINGING HIGH SCHOOL STUDENT

Background

During her sophomore year of high school, student Cindy formed a close friendship with classmate Andrew, who initially found her to be fun, intense, and full of energy, as if they were the stars of their own movie. However, their relationship began to feel increasingly one-sided and emotionally draining over time. Cindy had a tendency to make everything revolve around her. When Andrew shared his struggles, Cindy would always one-up him with her own problems, which seemed to be even worse. And whenever Andrew tried to focus on himself, Cindy would pull him back in with emotional manipulation, often through tears.

Cindy's home life was complicated. Her younger brother had a serious physical condition, causing her parents to be mostly focused on him. Meanwhile, her grandmother, who had lived with them for years, had been diagnosed with personality disorders. Although Cindy never spoke about it directly, it became clear that she often felt invisible in her family. This sense of neglect seemed to fuel her behavior.

At first, Andrew didn't mind being Cindy's go-to person. But over time, the emotional burden became overwhelming. Cindy would send frantic messages at all hours—crying over seemingly small issues, like an argument with a teacher or a bad grade. If Andrew didn't reply immediately, Cindy would send more texts or call repeatedly. Andrew, afraid of ignoring her, constantly felt the weight of Cindy's emotional needs.

The most concerning part was Cindy's self-harm. She would occasionally send pictures of cuts or hint at doing something worse, leaving Andrew in constant fear that if he ignored her, something serious might happen. No matter how much attention and care Andrew gave, it never seemed to be enough. If boundaries were set, Cindy would guilt-trip Andrew, claiming he was the only person who hadn't abandoned her. Eventually, the emotional demands took their toll, and Andrew realized that while he wanted to help Cindy, he wasn't equipped to do so. As a high school student, he struggled to balance his own life while trying to manage Cindy's needs.

Step 1: Setting Limits

Andrew: [Texting Cindy] Hey, I just got back from studying, I'm really tired. Can we talk tomorrow?

Cindy: [Texting back almost immediately] I can't believe you're ignoring me right now. I really need you. Everything is falling apart. I can't handle this on my own.

Andrew: I'm not ignoring you, Cindy. I just need to rest. I have a test tomorrow, and I'm drained.

Cindy: [Texting again] Well, I guess I'm just too much for you. I've been crying for hours, and you're too busy to even reply. I don't know who else to turn to. You're the only one who ever listens.

Andrew: I do listen, Cindy. I care, but I'm overwhelmed too. You need to take care of yourself as well. Please, try to talk to someone else if you can.

Cindy: [Texting with more urgency] No one else cares. I'm all alone. I just... I don't know what to do. Everything feels like it's crashing down. [Sends picture of her arm with cuts on it]

Andrew: [Feeling panic rise] Cindy, what's going on? Please tell me you're okay. You need to get help. I can't keep doing this.

Cindy: [Texting back quickly] You're the only one who gets me. I'm not sure I can do this anymore. If you don't reply, I'll just make it worse.

Despite Andrew expressing his need for rest and setting boundaries, Cindy disregarded his requests and continued to bombard him with messages. When he attempted to establish limits, like asking her to seek help from someone else, Cindy reacted with emotional accusations and guilt, undermining his boundaries. She completely disregarded Andrew's own needs, such as his need for rest and emotional space, and made her problems the center of their relationship, ignoring the fact that Andrew also had his own responsibilities and emotions to manage. Furthermore, Cindy framed herself as a victim, making statements like "No one else cares" and "Everyone always abandons me," which shifts the responsibility for her emotional well-being entirely onto Andrew. This behavior prevents her from taking responsibility for seeking appropriate help and creates a one-sided dynamic where Andrew is expected to "fix" everything.

Perhaps could set his limits more firmly, such as: "I can talk after 7 PM when I've finished studying" or "I can't answer texts late at night, and if it's urgent, you should contact someone else." Instead of just shutting her down, Andrew can offer alternative solutions, like suggesting she talk to a therapist for professional support, saying, "I think it would be helpful for you to talk to a therapist who can support you in ways I can't." When Cindy tries to guilt-trip or push his limits, he must stay firm while remaining compassionate, saying, "I understand that you're struggling, but my need for rest and space is important too."

Using "I" statements like "I feel overwhelmed when I don't have time for myself" helps avoid sounding accusatory while clearly stating his needs. Consistency is key; Andrew needs to reinforce his limits every time Cindy disregards them. He should acknowledge her feelings but prioritize his own mental health, expressing things like, "I know you're going through a lot, but I can't carry the responsibility of managing everything for you."

Andrew decided to try setting these firmer limits, but Cindy did not change her approach with him at all. In fact, she escalated her intensity. He realized that he had to impose some consequences in order to protect his own well-being.

Step 2: Imposing Consequences

Andrew thought about what kinds of consequences made sense for his situation. He considered telling Cindy that if she persists in disregarding his limits, he will have to take a break from their communication for a set period, like a day or two. If Cindy ignores his requests for space or sends multiple urgent messages despite Andrew asking her to wait, the consequence could be that he will stop responding to her messages for a certain period. This would help reinforce that her behavior has direct consequences, signaling that he won't tolerate being constantly bombarded with emotional crises.

If Cindy escalates her behavior with threats of self-harm,

Andrew should calmly, but firmly, express that while he cares for her, he cannot manage her emotional crises alone, and that professional help is necessary. He could set the consequence that if Cindy continues to use self-harm threats as a way to get attention, he will no longer engage with the situation until she seeks professional support. For example, Andrew could say, "If you continue to threaten self-harm, I will need you to reach out to a therapist or a trusted adult for support. I cannot manage this alone."

Andrew sought the support of a counselor and explained the situation. The counselor made it easy: "Impose your consequences of taking a day or two off and tell her that you won't be responding during that time. If she won't accept that limit and threatens self-harm, then contact me. There are actions I can take as a counselor when someone is threatening to hurt themselves. This is too big a burden for you to handle alone, especially as a high school student." Andrew decided to do this plan.

How Did Andrew Answer the Five Questions?

1. ***Is the consequence proportional to the limit I have set?***
   Yes. Calling the counselor when Cindy threatened to hurt herself totally fit the situation. Calling the police right away would have been too much and trying to handle it himself would have been too little.
2. ***Have I considered positive consequences as well as negative consequences?***
   Yes. Having Cindy talk to the counselor was actually a positive consequence rather than a negative consequence.
3. ***Is the consequence safe?***
   Yes. Talking to the counselor was safe and if she hung up the police would be called.

4. ***Am I ready to enforce my consequences?***
   Yes. He had talked to the counselor and would call the counselor if Cindy made any threats. He was desperate to get her some help and someone else involved who had more experience with situations like this.
5. ***Do I need to get help in imposing my consequence?***
   Yes. Andrew did the right thing by seeing a counselor about the situation. The counselor would help by talking to her. If she refused, then the counselor was going to call the police.

Andrew: "Cindy, I want you to know that I can't handle this, so I'm going to be taking two days off, without responding to your phone calls or texts."

She immediately said: "Then I'm going to hurt myself because you don't care and you're the only one I could count on. Now there's no one."

"Actually, there is," Andrew replied. "I'm talking to a counselor and I told him I would call him if you threatened to hurt yourself. Since you just did, I'm calling him now."

Cindy: "No, no! I'm not going to do anything. I was just saying that."

Andrew: "Then you need to tell him that. He's going to call you. I gave him your phone number and your mother's number. If you don't talk to him, then he will call the police. So please talk to him now. I care about you getting the support you need."

Andrew called the counselor, who called Cindy. (The counselor had gotten her mother's permission.) She answered his call and agreed to see a counselor with her mother that evening. Out of that meeting she agreed to get some ongoing counseling for herself where she would learn to manage her emotions better so they wouldn't run her life.

Step 2½: EAR Statement (or Not)

This was certainly a situation in which an EAR Statement was important. Andrew repeatedly told her he cared and that she needed to get some help because he couldn't handle it alone. The adults that she interacted with also gave her a lot of empathy, attention, and respect for her efforts to manage her own emotions more effectively.

Discussion

The relationship between Andrew and Cindy illustrates the challenges of managing emotional dependence and the difficulty of setting and maintaining boundaries in a one-sided friendship. Despite Andrew's efforts to provide support, Cindy's manipulative behaviors, overwhelming emotional needs, and disregard for Andrew's well-being created an unhealthy dynamic.

In this case, Andrew learned that he couldn't handle Cindy's intense emotions by himself and did the right thing to get some help. This turned out to be the best possible scenario because he went to someone who knew how to deal with teenage emotions: a counselor. This is an example of needing to get help for imposing consequences and getting it.

This type of situation is not that unusual in any close relationship, whether school friends, work friends, neighbor friends or otherwise. Occasionally, someone may want you to solve all their problems or to cling to you. This can be too much for any one person, and therefore it's important to be able to assert your boundaries or limits to protect your own mental health. Counselors are good people to go to for getting help in setting your limits and imposing consequences when necessary for your own emotional well-being.

Students in particular need to learn how to set limits and impose consequences, because their relationships with each other can be very close and intense, but also can get too close and intense for one of the people and learning how to back away can be tricky. One recommendation is to get to know people with a little bit of caution as you get closer, so that you don't have to suddenly back away or stop responding to phone calls and texts. The better people get at setting limits and imposing consequences, the easier it is to make friends without worrying that you will get overwhelmed.

[If you are or anyone you know is feeling in a crisis or threatening to hurt themselves, there are crisis help lines in most cities. And of course, 911 is available for emergencies.]

CONFLICT IN THE STUDENT GOVERNMENT

Background

Sarah, the newly elected President of the Greenfield University Students' Union (GUSU), faced a significant challenge when managing Mark, a fellow member of the Student Representative Council (SRC), who was underperforming in his role. Mark had been missing meetings, failing to complete tasks, and disruptive when he did attend, which affected the council's progress. To address this, Sarah initiated a Performance Improvement process to discuss his behavior.

During their first meeting, Mark became defensive and requested more details about his performance. Sarah initially focused too much on his past mistakes, which only increased the tension. Realizing this, she shifted her approach, using meeting agendas and EAR (Empathy, Attention, Respect) statements to guide the conversation and focus on solutions. Over time, Mark became more receptive and started improving his behavior, coming to meetings on time and completing tasks. But he still was a bit obnoxious during meetings themselves.

This experience taught Sarah valuable lessons in leadership and conflict resolution, emphasizing the importance of clear communication and understanding individual challenges. It also helped her build confidence in her ability to manage difficult situations.

Step 1: Setting Limits

Sarah (President): "Mark, I've noticed some tasks haven't been completed, and you've missed a few meetings. Can we talk about it?"

Mark (SRC Member): "What do you mean? You're just picking on me! Everyone else is doing the same thing, but I'm the one you're coming after!"

Sarah (President): "I'm not picking on you, Mark. We all have responsibilities, and I'm just trying to address the issue so we can work together. Can we talk about what's been getting in the way?"

Mark (SRC Member): "I don't need you telling me what to do. You're the one who doesn't understand. No one cares about the stuff I'm going through. Why should I care about this committee?"

Sarah realized that she needed to focus this meeting on Mark's problem behavior and the positive behavior she desired.

Sarah: "Mark, I'm concerned that during committee meetings you disrupt the flow of the meeting by interrupting people, bringing up topics that are not on the agreed-up Agenda, and being rude to people with insults about their intelligence and blaming them for problems that are actually group problems—not caused by one individual. None of this is helpful. You don't really seem to care about the work at all."

Mark: "Well, I'm just trying to point out the truth about people's stupidity."

Sarah: "What I mostly need you to do is to watch me and when I give a signal that you should back off, then I expect that to be sufficient. Otherwise, I may need to halt the meeting and take you aside, which would be embarrassing for both of us. Here, let me give you a copy of a Respectful Meeting Policy that I came across last week. I think this is what we need for our council."

Step 2: Imposing Consequences

Sarah showed Mark The Respectful Meeting Policy, which stated as follows:

"At ____ Company, much of our work is accomplished at meetings. In order to ensure the smooth, respectful and efficient management of meetings, the meeting chair shall manage the Agenda and the right of members to speak. On rare occasion, a meeting member may become disrespectful in communicating their information and opinions. In such a case, the meeting chair shall ask the meeting member to revise their manner of speech to be respectful. In the event that the meeting member does not thereafter speak respectfully, the chair may announce a short break or end the meeting, in the meeting chair's discretion. Other meeting members shall support the chair in making such decisions." (Eddy, 2024)

Mark: "Ok, I get it. I will be more respectful at meetings."

Mark struggled with holding his tongue at meetings, but he did succeed. Then he decided to quit the Council. He felt too confined and decided to get out of student government. He decided that he was going to start a band and focus on his musical career.

How Did Sarah Answer the Five Questions?

1. ***Is the consequence proportional to the limit I have set?*** *Yes. Halting the meeting if Mark was out of line was appropriate because he was disrupting it.*

2. ***Have I considered positive consequences as well as negative consequences?***
   No. Sarah just focused on having him back off, with negative consequences of removing him from meetings if necessary. She thought about positive consequences, but couldn't think of any.
3. ***Is the consequence safe?***
   Yes. Mark has no history of violence, so if he is excluded from a meeting that should be safe.
4. ***Am I ready to enforce my consequences?***
   Yes. Sarah is really frustrated, so she is motivated to control Mark and limit his damage to the Council.
5. ***Do I need to get help in imposing my consequence?***
   Yes. She will probably need support from the rest of the committee/council if she stops a meeting and tries to exclude Mark from a meeting.

The outcome of Mark quitting the Council was not that surprising. People who don't like limits especially don't like it when they are confronted on their own disruptive behavior.

Step 2½: EAR Statement (or Not)

Sarah should definitely use empathy, attention, and respect when setting limits with Mark. These qualities can help de-escalate the situation and maintain a professional tone, even when dealing with high-conflict behavior. Showing empathy can help Mark feel heard, while attention to his concerns demonstrates that Sarah is willing to listen, even if she's setting firm boundaries. Respect is crucial in maintaining the integrity of their professional relationship, even if Mark's behavior is challenging.

For example, Sarah could say, "I understand that you're frustrated, and I can see how this situation is important to you.

However, I need to be clear that the behavior you've been showing is not acceptable. I want to work with you to resolve this, but I need you to respect the boundaries we've set in place."

By combining empathy, attention, and respect with clear limits and consequences, Sarah can navigate the conversation more effectively, showing that she values the relationship but will not tolerate disruptive behavior.

However, even though she took this approach, Mark quit, perhaps to show that no one could tell him what to do. This may be a good learning experience for Mark or the beginning of a career of oppositional behavior. Only time will tell.

Discussion

The limits Sarah set with Mark may not work effectively due to his high-conflict personality, which often makes him resistant to authority and challenging to manage. People with this personality type may react defensively, escalate conflicts, or dismiss boundaries altogether, viewing them as attacks on their competence. Mark's emotional dysregulation and tendency to manipulate situations further complicate enforcement of limits. Additionally, if Sarah does not consistently follow through on the consequences, Mark might feel the limits are flexible and not serious. His ability to deflect blame or manipulate conversations can prevent meaningful change, requiring Sarah to adopt other strategies, such as involving third parties or seeking additional support, to manage the situation.

The fact that Mark quit the Council is not that unusual for high-conflict people in organizations. The feel too confined. When limits are more tightly set, they tend to rebel by fighting them or quitting. This is true in any committee, from student government groups to good paying jobs. They have a hard time deferring to others or the administrators of the group.

Conclusion

While this chapter focused on student conflicts in schools, these situations can arise in any group setting or work setting as well. The dismissiveness shown by Amelia's professor could also occur in a workplace with an arrogant supervisor or company boss. The same principles and 2½ steps would apply. Likewise, the intense friendship at school needing limits on Cindy could occur in a workplace or neighborhood or other setting. A disruptive council or committee member can occur in any volunteer group or even governing board, and they happen more often than most people know because these organizations keep it private. Regardless of the age of the people involved, the same basic principles apply: Set limits, impose consequences, and in about half the situations use an EAR Statement.

CHAPTER 10

AT WORK

Work usually involves ongoing relationships with the potential for misunderstandings, different expectations, and clashing personalities. Sometimes up to five generations may be working together in the same place. Rules and policies are always changing. Companies merge, are sold, or spin off divisions. Therefore, setting clear limits and having clear consequences for violating them is usually required. Many rules are not written down and just assumed. Setting limits is a common task for all organizations yet most managers and professionals are not experienced at or trained in setting limits and, especially, imposing consequences. This takes practice and a balance between being firm and showing empathy, attention, and respect.

Ideally, SLIC solutions will help organizations keep good employees and managers, even when they have difficulties from time to time. The goal is to facilitate a behavioral course correction rather than to fire everyone who makes a mistake or tolerate bad behavior while other good people leave.

THE NASTY MANAGER

Jill Jones was a mid-level manager for a high-tech company that hired people from many different cultural and national backgrounds. She herself was not born in the United States but arrived at a young age. She was very smart and, unfortunately, became very arrogant. In fact, it appeared that her arrogance was part of her way of coping with being different.

She did so well in her technical job that she was promoted to a management position. However, she soon got into trouble for sending emails that were disparaging to many of the employees she now supervised. "You're an idiot! You're doing it all wrong!" she would write.

"How did you ever get hired to work for this company?" "You should have had this project done yesterday! What are you, a snail?" and on and on. Somehow, Ms. Jones got the idea that by insulting her employees she was motivating them to do better. Instead, the employees complained to Human Resources, who sought consultation from the High Conflict Institute because of a recent training they had received.

"Should we fire her or just let her be?" they asked. "Will she get better?"

Step 1: Setting Limits

It was recommended that her supervisor have a meeting with Ms. Jones to set limits. "Let her know what words are okay and what words are not okay in some of her recent emails. Give her three coaching sessions with the BIFF method of email communication, using the *BIFF at Work* book which has thirty sample emails that are *brief, informative, friendly, and firm*. See if she can change her writing style and her speaking style."

We have given this advice in other circumstances as well. The only way to know if they can change is to give them a chance to change and see what happens. Of course, in some cases it may be too late to give the person that opportunity and consequences must be immediately imposed. But with Ms. Jones there was a glimmer of hope so it was worth a try.

Step 2: Imposing Consequences

In this case, it was determined that she should be informed of the consequence of losing her job if she didn't improve after three coaching sessions. They decided that the status quo was not tolerable for the company if she did not change.

Another option was considered and then abandoned. That was for her to return to her lower-level job where she had excelled because of her technical skills. Sometimes managers return to the job they had before, because they preferred it or simply were not good managers. However, in this case she had alienated so many of her employees that the company decided that if she didn't change she would need to leave for the sake of her department. If she did change how she communicated, then it was expected that she could heal those relationships.

How Did the Company Answer the Five Questions?

1. ***Is the consequence proportional to the limit I have set?***
   Yes. Ms. Jones had become a difficult manager who needed to change or leave.
2. ***Have I considered positive consequences as well as negative consequences?***
   Yes. The coaching is a positive consequence so that she can keep her job if she improves. If she doesn't, then she loses her job.
3. ***Is the consequence safe?***
   Yes. Unless she has indicated threats (in her words or behavior) against employees or the company, this consequence should be safe.
4. ***Are we ready to enforce our consequences?***
   Yes. It has reached a point of necessary change and we are ready to force the change, either in a positive or negative direction.

5. ***Do I need to get help in imposing my consequence?*** *Yes. The supervisor of Ms. Jones will need the backing of the company to enforce firing her if that becomes necessary.*

Step 2½: EAR Statement (or Not)

Ms. Jones has been a valued employee and may change enough to stay with the organization. Therefore, giving her motivating EAR Statements would be very important. Since she has an issue with arrogance in her personality, hearing that she is respected for some things could be especially helpful. This should not be exaggerated, but acknowledging her positive behaviors and talents may help in motivating her to improve.

Discussion

The outcome of the case of Jill Jones is not known. However, with coaching in similar situations in other organizations, about half of cases had employees and managers who were able to change their behavior enough to stay. In the other half of cases, employees and managers were so resistant to change that they were let go or just quit rather than being coached (which some viewed as an insult).

The question of whether to fire or keep high-conflict employees will never go away. However, in many organizations there are valued employees that they don't want to lose, but who are difficult. Many organizations have just tolerated the behavior and lost other valued employees because of it, especially if they worked under a high-conflict manager who was unrestrained. Other companies have simply fired the employee when there might have been some possibility of rehabilitation. Coaching as a consequence of troublesome behavior is a good option, as there is the possibility of improvement. If the employee knows that not doing the coaching or not changing their approach enough will lead to the consequence of being fired, they are often more motivated than if it is presented as simply a good idea. It's often the consequence that motivates the behavior change.

High Conflict Institute has two coaching methods. One is designed for employees in need of improving their conflict resolution skills or who simply want to improve their skills, known as *New Ways for Work*® coaching. The other method is for leaders and executives called *New Ways for Work for Leaders.*

THE DIFFICULT FORMER EMPLOYEE

Background

A 20-year county employee was disciplined and fired five years ago. After being let go, he repeatedly contacted four female county employees in hundreds of contacts over more than three years. "He frequently visits their offices and behaves in an abusive, harassing, aggressive and hostile manner." He claimed that the procedures where he worked were improper, but that no one would listen to him. However, the officials at his old department said that they paid attention and responded to any concerns that he would raise in numerous emails and phone calls.

Step 1: Setting Limits

The County wanted him to leave everyone alone and to stay away from his old worksite. Firing him was apparently insufficient. On at least three occasions, he came up to one of the workers as she walked from the building to her car in the parking lot. The employees changed their routines to protect themselves. The County hired armed security guards at the worksite. But these limits had little effect. The man appeared unstoppable.

Step 2: Imposing Consequences

This was a case in which setting more limits would require consequences. What should be done? The County decided to pursue a restraining order that included the following limits:

The former employee would stay 100 yards away from the four women's homes and workplaces

The former employee would be forbidden from visiting the County Administration Building and Operations Center.

He would no longer be allowed to attend Board of Supervisors meetings in person, although he could call in and submit written comments.

At court, the County got a temporary restraining order (TRO) granting the above requests. Then at the final "permanent restraining order" hearing three weeks later, the judge made the restraining order for five years, an extraordinary length of time. Violating a restraining order like this could land the person in jail.

How Did the County Answer the Five Questions?

1. ***Is the consequence proportional to the limit that we have requested?***
   Yes. The former employee was harassing and threatening employees. A restraining order narrowly designed to protect them was very appropriate.
2. ***Have we considered both positive and negative consequences?***
   Yes. The positive consequence is that he can stay out of jail by following the limits set in the restraining order. If not, the negative consequence is jail time.
3. ***Is the consequence safe?***
   Yes. A restraining order does not harm the restrained person; it just limits him.

4. ***Are we ready to enforce our consequences?***
   Yes. The County actually tolerated this behavior for three years, so its officials were very ready to enforce a consequence.
5. ***Do we need to get help in imposing our consequence?***
   Yes. The County and the women were unable to stop him with changed routines and security guards. So they needed help from the courts (and police, if necessary).

Would he follow it? In the County's petition to the court, they said his "behavior persists and continues to escalate. Moreover, he has repeatedly stated that he will ignore the cease-and-desist letters, will ignore any future restraining order, and is willing to be arrested."

However, a year later, the outcome appears to be that he complied with the restraining order and stayed away from the women and the forbidden county buildings. Since the order was made, there was no action involving the former employee that reached the public media, which would have happened if he had been arrested for violating the order.

Step 2½: EAR Statement (or Not)

This is the type of case where a stern setting of limits and imposing of consequences is clearly needed, so that an EAR Statement might have implied an opening for more harassment and manipulation. It is unknown whether the women, the County officials or the Court gave him any EAR Statements as they were setting limits, but by the time they were in court it appears unlikely.

Discussion

This is an extreme case of a former employee who appeared unstoppable. While this is very rare, there are people today who believe in their own isolated viewpoint without any objective evidence. This is a characteristic of high-conflict personalities that catches most people by surprise. Simple persuasion has no impact and setting ordinary limits has no impact, therefore significant consequences need to be imposed. This is a case that shows such a need and that this may have been an effective solution.

One thing that we have learned in dealing with high-conflict cases is to take limit-setting action sooner rather than later, because the person may never change and instead has to be stopped by employers or the courts. Once it is clear that one is dealing with a high-conflict person, giving more than one or two chances is likely to be pointless.

HIGH-STATUS HEALTHCARE PROFESSIONAL

Background

High-status professionals can occasionally be high-conflict people who need to have limits set and consequences imposed. While all occupations have some high-conflict people, healthcare, higher education, and nonprofit organizations are areas that particularly attract them because of the power, deference, and independence they are allowed. For this reason, organizations need to teach conflict resolution skills and actively set limits when professionals step out of bounds.

Over the past couple decades, the healthcare industry has gone through rapid changes and is required by accrediting organizations to teach conflict resolution skills, even to their doctors. In this hypothetical example inspired by real events, a surgeon is confronted with behavior that needs to be changed. The following dialog is taken from a video that High Conflict Institute uses in its workplace trainings.

HOSPITAL ADMINISTRATOR: "Good afternoon Dr. Star. Thank you for coming in today."

DR. STAR (slouches, spreading out over two chairs): "Why am I here? You know I've got a very busy surgery schedule and just finished my day."

ADMIN: "Ok, I'll get right to the point. We value your time and your work is a very important part of this hospital."

DR. STAR: "You're damn straight it is. I bring in about 10 million a year in surgeries for this hospital."

ADMIN: "You're absolutely right and we want you to be happy. We are very pleased with the quality of your surgeries, and the world is better off for all the people you have helped – whose lives you have saved!"

Step 1: Setting Limits

ADMIN (continues): "The Medical Director asked me to speak with you about a problem with the nursing staff. Have you heard about any problems with the nursing staff?"

DR. STAR: "Oh, they're always complaining about something. What is it this time?"

ADMIN: "Communication. They're telling us that nurses are quitting because of how you communicate with them. But that's something that can easily be improved. I don't know if you've heard, but many healthcare systems are hiring physician coaches to help their best doctors with their communication skills. We want you to meet with one of these coaches."

DR. STAR (sits up): "I won't do it. What can they teach me? What are they (sneers) – social workers?"

ADMIN: "Some are social workers and other professionals who all specialize in working with doctors and managers in healthcare. They understand the pressures you're under and they have worked with many doctors who say they liked them – that they really helped them."

DR. STAR: "What do the nurses complain about – specifically?"

ADMIN: "That you yell at them and sometimes throw

things at them in the operating room. That you scream that they're idiots. It's hard to keep nurses when that happens – and it's several that have told us this. But we respect you so much that we think you can change this behavior."

Step 2: Imposing Consequences

ADMIN (continues): "Otherwise, the Medical Director tells me there will need to be a Board meeting about you – and we're hoping to avoid that. And we hope you'll want to avoid that too. So what do you say? Can we get you started with the physician coaching within the next 7 days?"

DR. STAR: "How long do I need to go to this (sneers) 'physician coaching?'"

ADMIN: "It's at least six weekly sessions, but you can decide if you want more. It's up to you and the coach. We just get a notice you completed six sessions. We don't hear what you talk about at all. It's all strictly confidential. We'll just notice if things get better with the nurses. I can give you the names of three coaches. The one you pick will notify me when you begin and when you have completed six sessions. I think you'll find it really helpful. The other doctors have said that it's helped make things easier for themselves as well as the staff around them."

DR. STAR (leans over): "Give me the list."

ADMIN gives him the list and he walks out without saying another word.

How Did the Administrator Answer the Five Questions?

1. ***Is the consequence proportional to the limit that I have set?***
   Yes. Coaching for good staff relations is proportional to his bad communication skills.
2. ***Have I considered both positive and negative consequences?***

Yes. If the surgeon does the coaching and improves behavior, then he can keep his job and be mostly left alone by the administration. But if he refuses or does not change, then there will be a Board meeting about him.

3. ***Is the consequence safe?***
   Yes. Getting coaching should be very safe.
4. ***Is she ready to enforce our consequences?***
   Yes. She was very well-prepared and knew that if there was no change, bigger problems would result.
5. ***Does she need help in imposing the hospital's consequence?***
   Yes. The Director is already backing her up.

Step 2½: EAR Statement (or Not)

It's clear from the start that the hospital administrator wants Dr. Star to feel valued and open to the limits that are going to be set. Therefore, she really emphasized *respect* in her opening comments, and he seemed to like that. With a person like this who appears arrogant, it is probably not a good idea to emphasize or even mention words that show empathy, because he will probably manipulate or challenge them something like this: "Care about me? You don't care about me. You just want the money I bring in to the hospital!" This could distract from setting the limits and threatening the consequences.

Discussion

In this case, ordinary civil behavior should have been already understood (not throwing things in the Operating Room, not calling nurses idiots, etc.). Therefore, the initial limits were already set. The focus became the immediate consequence of needing to go through coaching. If that did not happen, then the bigger consequence of having a Board meeting about the surgeon would occur. Threatening that seemed to be the motivating factor. Soon after that he accepted the requirement of doing the coaching. It often helps to have a bigger consequence pending in case the smaller consequence is ignored.

These general principles can be applied to many types of professionals and executives who may be acting badly. Every occupation has them. In general, many see themselves as very superior to those they work with. The temptation is to try to criticize their behavior and attitude, to bring them down a bit. This generally does not work and can be counter-productive. It's better to treat them with respect, but don't overdo it.

Conclusion

These examples are just three at random that demonstrate the two and a half steps, rather than attempting to be a comprehensive text of workplace conflicts needing limits and consequences. But they do demonstrate three basic principles: 1) Require coaching as a way of assessing whether to fire or keep an employee. 2) Some people are almost immune to limits, so if you are dealing with someone with questionable behavior don't give them endless chances. See if they will make the effort to change fairly soon, otherwise you will get manipulated and waste a lot of time and resources feeling frustrated. 3) Be prepared for pushback from the person you are setting limits on, so think of as many of their challenges beforehand so that you have ready responses. Also, as stated many times before, practice what you will say with someone else a couple days ahead of time.

CHAPTER 11

IN BUSINESS

The business world today is significantly dominated by a handful of gigantic tech companies: including Google, Apple, Meta, Microsoft, Amazon and others. Most of us use them for some of our business as well as personal use. However, even though they are huge, they still have to follow the law and allow realistic competition in creating and distributing technology. With that in mind, there are frequently large lawsuits against most of these companies for unfair competition practices. In this chapter we will look at one example out of many that demonstrates the variety of consequences that can be imposed on large companies that most of us do business with.

The second example highlights a client-consultant dispute where a client initially praised the work but soon reversed course, launching personal attacks and demanding a refund despite all contractual deliverables being met. This case shows the importance of setting limits and imposing consequences while using mediation to manage emotional escalation and preserving professional dignity.

EPIC GAMES V. GOOGLE

In 2020, Epic Games filed lawsuits against both Apple and Google after they each removed Fortnite from their app stores. This happened after Epic's attempt to have their own payment system built into its app rather than being forced to get paid through Apple or Google and paying them a 30% commission for using their payment systems. The Apple case was decided by a District Court judge, who found Apple guilty of unfair competition and issued an injunction preventing it from requiring their payment system in the future.

The Google lawsuit was combined with some other lawsuits against it, which we will discuss here. This information is drawn from the 9th Circuit Court of Appeals published opinion in July 2025: *Epic Games v. Google* (see citation under References at the end of this book).

Step 1: Setting Limits

There have been antitrust laws on the books for decades against companies that unfairly block competition or manipulate competition so that consumers have fewer choices. So legally the limits have been set and in place for years. However, new companies sometimes come in and take over a market, pushing everyone else out of the business. When Google began, there were few search engines, although Yahoo had been around for years. But Google grew so big, so fast that they squeezed other companies. They also took advantage of smaller companies by requiring them to use their payment system instead of their own.

In the case of Epic Games v. Google, the unanimous jury found in favor of Epic. The two limits that Google had violated were 1) that it wouldn't allow Epic to be obtained through its app store and 2) the required "tying in" of in-app payments to Google's "Google Play Billing" system. The next question was: What should the consequences be?

Step 2: Imposing Consequences

The court decided to impose a variety of consequences restraining Google's practices:

Prohibition of Anticompetitive Arrangements: The injunction bars Google from continuing in certain conduct that was found to be anticompetitive by the jury, such as providing revenue-sharing or various other benefits to app distributors, developers, OEMs, or carriers in exchange for advantaging the Play Store or Google Play Billing, or for excluding rival app stores.

Catalog Access Remedy: The injunction mandates that Google permit third-party Android app stores to access and themselves distribute the Google Play Store's catalog of apps, enabling rival stores to offer users a comparable library of software products.

App Store Distribution Remedy: The injunction mandates that Google distribute third-party Android app stores through the Play Store, removing barriers that previously locked out competitors.

Technical Committee Oversight: The injunction establishes a three-person Technical Committee, with members selected by both parties, to oversee implementation of the newly mandated functions and resolve technical disputes, with the district court retaining ultimate authority.

In this case, Google appealed the jury's decision to the Court of Appeals (Ninth Circuit), which has handled many high-tech disputes. The Court of Appeals affirmed (upheld) the jury's decision and wrote a detailed opinion about it which may influence future cases. The decision said what Google was not allowed to do (prohibitory injunctions) as well as what it must do (affirmative steps to open up the market).

Since the written opinion was by the Court of Appeals, a review of it suggests the following answers to the five questions.

How Did the Court Answer the Five Questions?

1. ***Is the consequence proportional to the limit that the antitrust law set?***
   Yes. The decision carefully fit the consequences to the specific actions of Google by restraining Google from the same behavior in the future and opening itself back up to Epic Games.
2. ***Have we considered both positive and negative consequences?***
   No. In this case it was appropriate to focus just on negative consequences since it was not going to seriously hurt Google's huge business.
3. ***Is the consequence safe?***
   Yes. It's just business decisions.
4. ***Are we ready to enforce our consequences?***
   Yes. That's the job of the Court of Appeals and they did their job.
5. ***Do we need help in imposing our consequence?***
   Yes. This case was unusual in that the Court required the establishment of "Technical Committee Oversight," which involved a three-person committee to oversee the implementation of the requirements of the court order; essentially making sure the consequences were properly followed.

Step 2½: EAR Statement (or Not)

This was clearly a business dispute in somewhat new areas of the law, so that soothing feelings and motivating individual behavior change were not really the issue. However, we don't know what the business relationship of the parties was or is, so it's possible that EAR Statements were made or should have been made to smooth out their future business relationship.

Whether the Court of Appeals made EAR Statements during the case is unknown without reading all the transcripts of the hearings.

Discussion

This case was a good example of how even big businesses need to have limits set and that consequences can be imposed on them for violating existing laws. It was unusual in that the Court not only restrained the company from past behavior but also required it to perform mandatory future behavior. Overall, these consequences were seen as ways to "pry open to competition a market that has been closed by defendants' illegal restraints." There did not appear to be financial penalties, but instead Google was forced to work with Epic Games again so that people could get the app from Google and Epic could make money without giving Google 30%.

CONSULTANT REPUTATION DISPUTE

Background

Anna, a market research consultant with an excellent reputation, was hired by a startup to deliver a detailed consumer behavior report. She was chosen specifically for her strong track record and outstanding ratings from past clients. The project scope included a final report, data analysis, and a presentation—all of which Anna completed on time and in full, in accordance with the signed contract.

Initially, the client was thrilled. They posted a public 5-star review praising Anna's work, gave her a generous bonus, and expressed interest in working together again. However, within days the situation reversed dramatically. Anna was unavailable for two days and slow in returning a phone call. The client apparently felt abandoned (some high-conflict people do have sudden reversals of attitude) and began personally attacking

Anna, discrediting her qualifications, and questioning the accuracy of her work—despite having already approved all deliverables. They demanded a full refund and posted a follow-up public review complaining that Anna's work was incomplete and substandard.

Step 1: Setting Limits

Recognizing that the client's behavior had shifted from professional disagreement to personal attack, Anna set clear limits. She communicated in writing that unfounded accusations and personal insults were unacceptable and would not be tolerated. She requested that any concerns be presented respectfully, with specific evidence tied to the agreed scope of work. She also reminded the client of her history of satisfied customers and the fact that all contract obligations had been met.

Her goal was to shift the conversation back to objective, evidence-based discussion and to protect both her professional reputation and her mental health.

Step 2: Imposing Consequences

When the client continued making emotional outbursts and unreasonable demands, Anna decided to stop direct communication and sought the services of a mediator. She threatened to sue the client for defamation because of the accusation that she did not complete the work when in fact the client had put in writing that it had been completed. Anna hoped that the mediation would make a lawsuit unnecessary. She stopped communicating directly with the client and referred all further contact to wait until the mediation. She organized detailed documentation—including her contract, delivery receipts, the original 5-star review, the bonus payment, and testimonials from other clients—to demonstrate both the quality of her work and her fulfillment of all obligations.

The consequence for the client was the loss of direct access to Anna, and the requirement to address all issues through formal dispute resolution channels. The additional threatened consequence was a lawsuit for defamation because of her false second public review.

How Did Anna Answer the Five Questions?

1. ***Is the consequence proportional to the limit set?***
   Yes. Limiting communication and requiring evidence was a reasonable response to personal attacks and baseless claims. If the mediation wasn't successful, then a lawsuit for defamation would be appropriate.
2. ***Have both positive and negative consequences been considered?***
   Yes. The positive consequence was the client's continued opportunity to resolve the dispute through mediation. The negative was the loss of direct access and the shift to a formal process if hostility continued, including a possible lawsuit.
3. ***Is the consequence safe?***
   Yes. Redirecting communications through a neutral third party reduced personal stress and avoided further verbal harassment.
4. ***Is she ready to enforce the consequence?***
   Yes. Anna maintained the no-direct-contact rule consistently. She also prepared her documentation for the mediation with the possibility of using the same documentation in a lawsuit if necessary, without delay.
5. ***Does she need help in imposing the consequence?***
   Yes. She sought the assistance of a mediator. She also was willing to use the court system if necessary with a defamation lawsuit.

Outcome: In the mediation, the client apologized to Anna for reacting so strongly. She had family troubles that week and felt abandoned by Anna not calling her back until a few days later. She agreed to write another public review clarifying that Anna had done all she was expected to do. Anna accepted her apology and agreed that she would not file a defamation lawsuit.

Step 2½: EAR Statement (or Not)

In the mediation, Anna was reluctant to offer empathy-based statements, as these could have been misinterpreted as agreement with the unfounded criticism. Instead, she kept her communications brief, factual, and respectful—avoiding unnecessary emotional engagement while maintaining professionalism. However, after the client apologized and discussed writing another review, Anna did give her some empathy (for going through a hard time that week) and respect (for being able to admit she had over-reacted). Her EAR Statements probably helped the client remain calm and responsible.

Discussion

This case illustrates that even highly satisfied clients can abruptly turn hostile, sometimes for reasons unrelated to the quality of work delivered. For independent professionals, it is critical to have a plan for when the conversation moves from professional disagreement to personal attack. Anna's approach—setting clear limits, enforcing consequences, and documenting every step—protected her professional reputation and mental well-being.

The lesson is that respect must be a non-negotiable condition in any professional relationship. While evidence and facts form the backbone of a defense in disputes, controlling the method and tone of communication can prevent further harm.

Conclusion

From a large public high-tech company to an individual professional, reputation is a valuable asset that must be actively protected. Google was willing to risk getting a reputation as a bully by shutting out Epic Games, so the court had to intervene and impose consequences. Anna's experience shows that combining firmness with professionalism, relying on documented evidence, and engaging neutral third parties when needed can prevent damaging escalation. Setting limits is only half the work. In both cases it took being prepared to follow through with proportional, enforceable consequences in order to maintain credibility and resilience in the long term.

CHAPTER 12

GOVERNMENT

Government workplaces come with their own set of unique pressures—rigid hierarchies, high public accountability, and policies that often intersect with ethical, legal, and political tensions. While many civil servants enter government roles with a strong sense of purpose, interpersonal conflicts can still arise, particularly when professional expectations clash with personal loyalties, political ideologies, or unclear boundaries.

This chapter focuses on two examples of workplace conflict within fictional government departments in imaginary countries. These examples show how setting clear limits and enforcing fair consequences is essential—even in systems designed to uphold fairness and order.

THE GOVERNMENT WHISTLEBLOWER

Background

In the fictional country of Norvana, the Ministry of Waterworks is responsible for regulating water quality and infrastructure across the country. Two early-career civil servants, Amira and Soren, both in their mid-20s, joined the Ministry through a prestigious national fellowship. They worked closely on a regional clean-water initiative and quickly became close colleagues and friends, often grabbing lunch together and covering for each other during tight deadlines.

A year into the job, Amira discovered that a subcontractor hired by their department was falsifying water safety data in rural communities. She brought the issue to their supervisor, who dismissed her concerns. After gathering documentation and reviewing internal policy, Amira confidentially submitted a report to the Office of Government Integrity, Norvana's whistleblower protection body.

Weeks later, Amira began noticing subtle retaliation: she was left off team emails, excluded from key meetings, and given low-impact assignments. Soren, once a close confidant, distanced himself. Eventually, Amira learned that Soren had informed their supervisor about her whistleblower complaint—even though she had asked him not to share anything.

Step 1: Setting Limits

Hurt and feeling betrayed, Amira met privately with Soren.

Amira: "Soren, I need to talk about something serious. I know you told our supervisor about my whistleblower report—I was warned it might happen. But I need you to understand that wasn't your place."

Soren: "I thought you were making a mistake. Reporting outside the chain could get you blacklisted. I thought I was protecting you."

Amira: "You didn't protect me—you exposed me. I trusted you, and you broke confidentiality. Whether you agreed with my decision or not, it wasn't yours to share. I can't trust you with sensitive conversations anymore, and I won't be including you in future planning discussions unless we rebuild that trust. If I see any more signs of retaliation or hearsay tied back to you, I'll be filing an additional report."

Soren: "I get that you're upset. I didn't mean to make things worse."

Amira: "I'm not just upset—I'm serious. This is my job, and this is government integrity. We both swore an oath."

Amira followed up with a memo to herself documenting the conversation, in case further retaliation occurred.

Step 2: Imposing Consequences

Two weeks later, Amira found out from another colleague that Soren had shared her private concerns again—this time claiming Amira "was overreacting" and "risked the department's funding." Amira reported this to the Office of Government Integrity.

Within a week, the agency began a formal inquiry into retaliatory behavior within the department. Soren was called in for questioning, and the Ministry's Human Resources Office issued a written warning for breaching peer confidentiality during an active whistleblower protection process. He was reassigned to a non-collaborative role pending further review.

Amira was offered a transfer to a different policy team and chose to take it. She documented every step and received guidance from a legal liaison to ensure she stayed within protocol.

How Did Amira Answer the Five Questions?

1. ***Is the consequence proportional to the limit I have set?***
   Yes. She gave Soren a clear warning after the first breach and escalated after the second.
2. ***Have I considered both positive and negative consequences?***
   Yes. Amira set a limit and gave Soren a chance to change. If he had followed her request to keep things confidential, no action would have been taken. Reporting retaliation was her last resort

3. ***Is the consequence safe?***
   Yes. She followed legal whistleblower protocols and documented her actions properly.
4. ***Am I ready to enforce my consequence?***
   Yes. Amira clearly communicated her limits and followed through with official channels.
5. ***Does she need help in imposing the consequence?***
   Yes. She relied on the Office of Government Integrity and internal HR to enforce protections.

Outcome: How Did Soren Respond? Depending on his personality, there tend to be at least three outcomes in these types of situations.

A. Regretful but late Soren: After the investigation, Soren sent a private apology: "I should have respected your decision. I acted out of fear, not integrity. I hope someday you'll forgive me." They remained distant but cordial.

B. Defensive Soren: Soren blamed Amira for his demotion, telling others she "couldn't handle disagreement." The trust was broken, and they avoided each other entirely.

C. Vindictive Soren: Soren retaliated further by spreading rumors until HR intervened again. His contract was eventually not renewed.

Step 2½: EAR Statement (or Not)

Amira attempted a respectful but firm tone in her confrontation:

Empathy: "I get that you thought you were helping."

Attention: "Tell me what you were thinking. I want to understand."

Respect: Amira just focused on empathy and attention in this case and that was sufficient..

She kept her tone serious and direct, balancing professionalism with justified emotion.

Discussion

This example highlights the challenges of loyalty, integrity, and accountability within government systems. Amira learned to prioritize ethical responsibilities over personal comfort—even when it meant standing alone. Soren's betrayal reflected a broader cultural issue: fear of conflict or whistleblowing often leads people to protect institutions over truth.

This case reinforces how limits and follow-through are essential—even (and especially) in government workplaces where stakes are high and friendships can complicate professional duties.

POLITICAL CONFLICTS IN A GOVERNMENT AGENCY

Background

In the Federal Republic of Veridia, the Department of National Development (DND) employs civil servants from a variety of political backgrounds. Two policy analysts, Lena and Marcus, both new hires and former university classmates, have been assigned to the same team to draft a new infrastructure bill.

Lena identifies as a progressive liberal and advocates for green infrastructure and social equity. In contrast, Marcus is a conservative who prioritizes economic growth and advocates for limited government spending. Their differing views frequently come to light during team meetings, often escalating into heated debates that disrupt the workflow.

While political diversity is valued, their regular clashes have created discomfort among coworkers and delayed progress on the bill.

Step 1: Setting Limits

The team leader, Mr. Garin, called Lena and Marcus for a private discussion:

"Lena, Marcus, I appreciate your passion, but your disagreements are impacting team productivity. We need respectful, professional dialogue focused on policy outcomes, not political arguments. From now on, personal political views should be set aside during meetings. If you have concerns, present them factually and respectfully. If this behavior continues, I will have to involve HR for mediation and possible disciplinary action."

Both nodded, acknowledging the importance of professionalism.

Step 2: Imposing Consequences

Despite the warning, during the next meeting, Marcus interrupted Lena multiple times and made dismissive remarks about her proposals, leading to an argument in front of other team members.

Mr. Garin immediately paused the meeting and sent Marcus a formal written warning citing "unprofessional conduct detrimental to team cohesion." Marcus was required to attend a conflict resolution workshop and meet weekly with a mentor to improve his workplace communication.

How Did Mr. Garin Answer the Five Questions?

1. ***Is the consequence proportional?***
   Yes. A formal warning and training are appropriate responses after initial verbal warnings.
2. ***Have I considered positive and negative consequences?***
   Yes. Training and mentoring offer support (positive), while the warning is a negative consequence.
3. ***Is the consequence safe?***
   Yes. The approach maintains a professional environment and avoids escalation.

4. ***Am I ready to enforce my consequence?***
   Yes. Mr. Garin acted promptly after the rule violation.
5. ***Do I need help in imposing my consequence?***
   Yes. HR is involved to provide mediation and training resources.

Step 2½: EAR Statement (or Not)

When issuing the warning, Mr. Garin said:

"I understand political beliefs are deeply personal and important to you both. I respect your commitment to your values. However, the workplace must remain a space for respectful collaboration. We want to support your growth here and ensure the team can work effectively."

Discussion

This example illustrates how political differences can disrupt harmony in the workplace, particularly in government agencies where diverse opinions are prevalent. Establishing clear behavior guidelines, enforcing consequences for inappropriate actions, and promoting respectful communication are essential for maintaining professional standards and ensuring effective teamwork. Additionally, involving Human Resources for support and training can provide a constructive path forward.

In this case, Mr. Garin, the Team Leader, took quick action as soon as the conflict broke out in the open between Lena and Marcus. This is essential for people chairing meetings anywhere, otherwise the conflict can just spiral out of control. People chairing meetings in this day and age need to be prepared to intervene. We recommend adopting the following Respectful Meeting Policy, which encourages meeting chairpersons to stop meetings when necessary to maintain civility.

"At ____ organization, much of our work is accomplished at meetings. In order to ensure the smooth, respectful and efficient management of meetings, the meeting chair shall manage the Agenda and the right of members to speak. On rare occasion, a meeting member may become disrespectful in communicating their information and opinions. In such a case, the meeting chair shall ask the meeting member to revise their manner of speech to be respectful. In the event that the meeting member does not thereafter speak respectfully, the chair may announce a short break or end the meeting, in the meeting chair's discretion. Other meeting members shall support the chair in making such decisions." (Eddy, 2024)

After Mr. Garin stopped the meeting, he met with the two people in conflict. This helps provide structure and gives people a chance to change. Potentially high-conflict people need more structure, then they are more likely to act responsibly and succeed.

Conclusion

These two examples demonstrate common workplace dynamics and the need for limits and consequences. They also show some of the unique issues of government agencies, including the need to protect whistle-blowers for government accountability and keeping political differences at bay as much as possible among the workforce.

CHAPTER 13

SOCIAL MEDIA

The pervasive nature of online platforms has fundamentally altered how individuals interact, creating both opportunities and challenges in the realm of social behavior. Within digital communities, the lines between acceptable and unacceptable conduct are often blurred, leading to situations where personal boundaries are violated and individuals are subjected to harmful actions. This chapter examines the crucial need for establishing clear limits and imposing appropriate consequences for online interactions. Whether it involves the exploitation of personal encounters or the experience of targeted harassment within online communities, the ability to assert control and protect oneself is essential. This analysis will focus on understanding the mechanisms by which individuals can reclaim their agency, address violations of privacy and consent, and contribute to the cultivation of a more respectful and accountable online environment. The core issue revolves around the power dynamics within online interactions and the necessity for both individuals and communities to develop strategies that promote ethical behavior and safeguard personal well-being.

BLOGGER OF BEVERLY HEIGHTS

In the sunny city of Beverly Heights, a place known for its vibrant streets and gorgeous residents and tourists, a local blogger named Jason had found his niche. Wearing a pair of Meta Ray-Ban glasses (feature camera, audio, and performance), he had a way of blending in while standing out. Not just another face in the crowd, Jason had mastered the art of observing the locals—particularly the beautiful women who filled the trendy cafes, organic food markets, and high-end boutiques. As a frequent visitor of this area, he knew all the hot spots where health-conscious, style-savvy women gathered.

Jason, however, wasn't there just to shop or enjoy a cup of overpriced green juice, he was there to spot, turn on his camera on his glasses, approach these women as if he were a shy, awkward guy attempting to navigate the intimidating world of dating.

"Can I get in line to be your boyfriend?" he would ask with a smile, his tone almost playful but laced with a hint of mockery.

Or sometimes, "Hi, you look so beautiful, what's your name?"

These were not romantic gestures or genuine attempts at conversation (he was already married). They were part of a plan—one that Jason was too eager to share with his growing online followers.

He'd secretly record these interactions, capturing the reactions of the women he approached. Some were confused, some laughed it off, and a few were outright uncomfortable. But Jason wasn't interested in the outcome of the interactions themselves. His goal was simple: post the footage online, title it "How to Hit on Women," and let his audience watch.

As the videos began to pile up on his social media, they quickly garnered attention. Jason's followers, mostly guys, ate it up. His boldness and his take on how to approach women in casual, often cringe-worthy ways fascinated them. And as the videos gained traction, so did the comments. Some followers commented with praise, saying how pretty the women were or how they'd love to try the same approach. Others, however, were more critical, commenting on which women were "pretty enough" to approach and which were "ugly." One day he ran into yet another woman, named Amy, who held a job at a huge local store selling beauty products. During her work break he came up to her and told her she looked beautiful and asked if he could get her number.

Jason (to Amy): "Hey, you look incredible. Can I get your number?"

Amy (hesitant):"Uh, I don't usually give my number to strangers, especially at my work break."

Jason (charming smile):"I get it, but I promise I'm not like the other guys. Just want to talk—no pressure."

Amy (sighing, softening):"I don't normally do this... but fine. Just don't be weird about it."

She gives him her number reluctantly.

Jason (grinning):"Thanks, I won't. Looking forward to talking."

Few days later, a longtime local shopper from the store, who had a good relationship with Amy, showed her Instagram.

Shopper (showing Amy the post):"Amy, look! I just saw you on Instagram."

Amy (shocked):"Are you kidding me?

In this situation, there were several problems. Jason's behavior violated social norms and could be harmful. Jason treats women as objects for his own amusement and social media content rather than engaging in genuine conversations. He did not get her consent to be videotaped and there are state laws against that in California, as well as store policies forbidding it.

Yet Jason recorded and posted these interactions without the women's consent, showcasing them as part of his "How to Hit on Women" series. This not only exploits women for the sake of his content but also potentially exposes them to ridicule, unwanted attention, and possible future harassment by strangers that saw it. By focusing on the awkward or uncomfortable reactions of women, Jason reinforces a power dynamic where women's normal boundaries are trivialized and violated to make them feel small or uncomfortable for his followers' amusement.

Jason's followers contribute to the problematic behavior by commenting on which women are "pretty enough" to approach, essentially reinforcing the objectification of women. Comments like these not only devalue women but encourage a toxic environment where appearance is the only factor that matters, contributing to low self-esteem and harmful stereotypes.

Step 1: Setting Limits

Upon discovering that Jason posted the interaction on Instagram, Amy immediately contacted him to demand the removal of the post. "I didn't consent to being recorded or posted online. Please remove the video immediately." Jason was resistant. She added: "You know this may violate the law, this may violate Instagram's policies, and it may violate the store's policies. You have three days to remove it while I look into my options. I hope that legal action won't be necessary. Just take it down!"

Step 2: Imposing Consequences

Amy talked to trusted individuals, including friends and coworkers, about the experience, because it left her feeling so uneasy. Discussing the situation helped reaffirm her rights and provided her with emotional support. Understanding the rules against this type of behavior empowered her to take the appropriate action.

Amy immediately reported the post to Instagram for violating her privacy and consent. Instagram has tools for reporting unwanted or harmful content, and Amy used these resources. She also reported the incident to her manager at the store and found out it violated store policies. She also found out that California law forbids recording conversations without the consent of both people involved, with certain exceptions.

Three days later, the video was still up on Jason's Instagram account.

"Jason, I have reported you to Instagram and to my store. You violated both of their policies. I spoke to a lawyer about this and found out that you may have to pay huge financial penalties for using my likeness for commercial purposes without my consent, allowing me to seek actual damages, statutory damages (minimum $750 per violation), your profits, and potentially punitive damages. You could also go to jail. You are in big trouble. I hope that it won't be necessary for me to hire that lawyer. He seemed real eager to take this case."

That afternoon the video was removed.

For more financial consequences, Amy considered that she could contact Jason's sponsors or advertisers if his blog is monetized, informing them that their brand is associated with unethical social media practices. She could also report the video on all platforms where it was shared (e.g., Instagram, YouTube, TikTok) to increase the chances of removal.

Amy also considered that she could work with local women's organizations, influencers, or journalists to raise awareness about online privacy violations and digital harassment without directly defaming Jason, which could discourage similar behavior in the future. She could also engage with local lawmakers to advocate for stricter privacy protections against non-consensual recordings. Additionally, if Jason has a professional career outside of blogging, Amy could bring his conduct to the attention of his employer. Many workplaces have codes of conduct that prohibit public harassment or unethical behavior.

Finally, by participating in community initiatives that educate others about consent and respectful online interactions, Amy could transform her negative experience into positive change while leveraging her network to support other women who have been similarly victimized, creating a collective voice against such invasive practices.

How Did Amy Answer the Five Questions?

1. ***Is the consequence proportional to the limit I have set?***
   Yes. The consequences are built into the laws and rules for improper online behavior.
2. ***Have I considered both positive and negative consequences?***
   Yes. In this case, the positive consequence is that Amy will not pursue legal action if Jason immediately takes down the video of her. Negative consequences are if he doesn't.
3. ***Is the consequence safe?***
   Yes. These consequences are designed to protect everyone.
4. ***Am I ready to enforce my consequence?***
   Yes. Amy is energized to put a stop to this video and hire a lawyer if necessary.
5. ***Do I need to get help in imposing my consequence?***
   Yes. She will pursue assistance from Instagram in enforcing their online policies, as well as assistance from her store, and if necessary a lawyer.

Step 2½: EAR Statement (or Not)

This is one of those cases where an EAR Statement is not advised and Amy did not use one. Jason appears to have a high-conflict personality that includes a lack of empathy and remorse. He has already demonstrated his ability to be deceitful and manipulative. Therefore, it was important for her to put all of her energy into setting her limits and imposing her consequences. It would be hard to find a reason to empathize with him or respect anything about his behavior. He has an extreme personality that must be stopped. Whatever the cause of his behavior, the most important thing was to stop it ASAP.

Discussion

Amy has a right to control her space, privacy, and online representation, and there are laws and policies to protect her and all citizens from online abuse. While Amy was shaken by seeing herself posted online, she was so angry that she took action to lodge complaints about it and make efforts to have it taken down immediately.

This is another example of a situation in which there are already limits set by lawmakers. The burden was on Jason to get permission to do what he did, not on her to set limits on his behavior. But she was able to use the limits set by Instagram, by her store, and by the law, and she backed them up with several possible consequences. This is another example of a case in which just setting limits ("please take it down") was insufficient and the credible threat of imposing consequences was necessary to get it taken down.

This is also a case in which we can see how the rules of civil interaction have changed and that policies are often slow to exist. The financial rewards for insensitive and abusive behavior online adds to the problem. Individuals need to be prepared to take action, as Amy did, to assert their personal limits and consequences. This also demonstrates that it often takes more than one person to impose consequences. On her own she wasn't able to get him to take it down, but when several others were involved he removed it.

This case study serves as a stark reminder of the ethical and legal challenges posed by the pervasive nature of social media. It underscores the need for individuals to be vigilant about their privacy and consent, and to understand their rights in the face of online exploitation. By empowering individuals like Amy with knowledge and support, we can foster a culture of respect and accountability in the digital realm. This case also highlights the potential for collective action and advocacy to drive meaningful change and create a safer, more equitable online experience for all.

ONLINE BULLYING OF ATHLETES

Background

The Winter Olympic competitions were expected to be a celebration of athletic achievement. However, months before the games, many athletes found themselves victims of harsh online bullying. Critics targeted their performances in pre-Olympic events and made derogatory remarks about their countries of origin. While athletes typically face intense scrutiny before major competitions, this time the attacks were more vicious and hurtful than ever.

This story highlights the damaging effects of online bullying on athletes and explores ways to address and prevent it. One such athlete was Elena Petrov, a figure skater from Veridonia. After competing in a 2023 skating event, she didn't perform as well as she had hoped. In response, a wave of cruel online comments followed. People criticized her skating technique, mocked her appearance, and even insulted her home country.

The bullying was organized, with groups of people sending Elena hurtful messages. The constant negativity took a toll on her mental and emotional well-being, causing her to feel anxious and stressed. Fortunately, Elena had a strong support system—her coach and a doctor helped her navigate these difficult emotions, and her fans, along with the Veridonia Figure Skating Association, expressed their unwavering support.

Examples of the Online Comments

User1 (Performance Criticism): "That routine was a mess, Elena. You're not Olympic-level."

User2 (Nationality-Based Harassment): "Veridonia always sends the weakest skaters. No surprise you messed up."

User3 (Personal Attack): "Your outfit was awful, and you looked so stuck-up. Try smiling next time."

User4 (Troll Campaign, using a fake profile): "#ElenaFail #VeridoniaLoser"

User5 (Performance Criticism): "You clearly didn't train enough. Disappointing."

These behaviors—dismissive criticism, harassment based on nationality, personal attacks, trolling, and unfounded assumptions—create a toxic environment that can significantly affect an athlete's mental health and well-being.

Step 1: Setting Limits

Elena considered whether replying to negative comments was necessary or beneficial for her well-being. She thought about whether it could be constructive or help others in similar situations if she chooses to respond calmly and assertively to educate people on the importance of respectful feedback, something like this: "I appreciate constructive criticism that helps me grow, but comments about my appearance or nationality are hurtful and unnecessary. Let's keep discussions focused on performance and improvement."

However, in many cases, engaging with online bullies can escalate the situation, causing more harm and giving the bullies the attention they seek. If responding feels like it would drain her energy or perpetuate the negativity, it's completely valid for Elena to ignore the comments, block users, or report harmful behavior instead. The most important thing is for Elena to protect her mental well-being while fostering a positive space for growth and support. Since she realized that their comments were meant to provoke her, she chose not to respond. She didn't have to set limits, because they were already in existence as standards of civility for adults who generally speak respectfully to each other. This is what all children learn growing up—or are supposed to learn.

Step 2: Imposing Consequences

Elena established clear and consistent consequences for this online bullying to protect herself and maintain a positive online space. First, she immediately reported and blocked anyone who engaged in this harmful behavior, preventing further access to her social media accounts. Additionally, she muted or removed individuals from online spaces she controlled, offering a temporary consequence for less severe offenses. She reported problematic behavior to platform moderators, especially when the bullying violated the platform's rules.

Elena encouraged her community to support one another and hold individuals accountable for their actions, fostering a culture of respect. She considered legal action, such as pursuing defamation claims or seeking a restraining order. However, she decided their behavior wasn't extreme enough. She knew that legal action would make her engage with the people she was trying to dis-engage from. By imposing these consequences of cutting them off, Elena felt that she created a safer environment for herself and others while reinforcing the importance of mutual respect online.

How Did Elena Answer the Five Questions?

1. ***Is the consequence proportional to the limit I have set?*** *Yes. By blocking and reporting the harassers' behavior and not responding she simply prevented them from their harassing behavior.*

2. ***Have I considered both positive and negative consequences?***
   No. In this case, Elena decided that she needed to just focus on the negative consequences of prevention.
3. ***Is the consequence safe?***
   Yes. Cutting them off did not appear to pose a risk and no one had made any violent threats.
4. ***Am I ready to enforce my consequence?***
   Yes. She immediately blocked and reported them.
5. ***Do I need to get help in imposing my consequence?***
   Yes. By blocking and reporting these trolls, the social media moderators would take it from there.

Step 2½: EAR Statement (or Not)

Elena chose not to give the online trolls any EAR Statements. They had already demonstrated highly insensitive behavior and seemed like they would manipulate anything she said. They already said she was "weak" and a "loser." As with the prior case, she decided to focus on being clear and firm with her consequences.

Discussion

The anonymity of the internet allows individuals to engage in harmful behavior without facing direct consequences, making it easier for bullies to target others without fear of reprisal. Responding to negativity, even with calm and assertive statements, can sometimes escalate the situation, as bullies may continue or intensify their attacks if they feel empowered by attention. Instead, Elena wisely chose to avoid responding and instead blocked and reported these harassers. However, sometimes social media platforms often fail to consistently enforce their own rules, and users can bypass reporting systems by creating new accounts or using different tactics. In this case, they left her alone after she blocked them.

After the Olympics were over, Elena and her support team actively engaged in communicating about bullies to others. This involved using public statements, social media campaigns, and interviews to raise awareness about the impact of online bullying. They educated fans and the public about the importance of respectful behavior and the effects of harassment on athletes. Elena shared her personal story and experiences to foster empathy and understanding, humanizing the issue and garnering support from the wider community. By using various communication channels, they aimed to create a broader understanding of the problem and encourage positive change.

Once again, similar to the first case in this chapter, Elena's harassers appeared to be high-conflict people who lacked empathy and remorse for their actions. Realizing this helps people focus on setting limits and imposing consequences, rather than wasting time trying to persuade such high-conflict people to act differently or giving them too much empathy. She realized that EAR Statements would be manipulated in this case and decided to leave them out of any discussions. Lack of active enforcement of platform rules makes it difficult to eliminate online bullying entirely. Although setting limits and imposing consequences are necessary, they may not always be enough to halt the harmful behavior. This emphasizes the importance of support systems—like coaches, fans, and professional help—in managing the emotional toll that online bullying can cause.

Conclusion

Online behavior is one of the most difficult issues of today as it is very hard to seriously impose consequences on it and anonymous bullies can have a field day. However, pressure on internet companies and governments to impose more controls will eventually be necessary. In the meantime, everyone needs to have a healthy skepticism about who they are dealing with online and everyone needs to learn to use the limits that we do have today to personally block and report high-conflict behavior.

In the first case in this chapter, we saw that a stranger can set up a situation in which they harass another person and put it on the internet. However, there are already laws about this and people need to learn what they can do to protect themselves. Getting help in important as it often takes more than one person to stop a bully.

In the second case, an Olympic athlete was harassed on line at a very vulnerable time as she was getting ready to compete in the Olympic games. While her consequences were limited, by blocking her harassers and not suing them, she was able to let the comments go and not get involved in any larger way. This helped her mental health and she did the best she could.

Learn the rules and your rights online, as they are constantly changing. In addition to these individual strategies, the broader community's support plays a crucial role in fostering respect and understanding. Public education campaigns and social media activism can raise awareness and create a safer, more positive online environment.

CHAPTER 14

PROFESSIONAL SITUATIONS

There are many professionals providing services to clients in many different settings today. Whether someone is a professional providing home repairs, financial services, legal services, healthcare, higher education, or a multitude of other services, they will need to manage communication with their clients, especially anxious clients. This chapter addresses setting limits on communication. It also addresses setting limits on client behavior when it deviates from the norms and legal standards.

ANXIOUS THERAPY CLIENTS

Background

Dr. Wilson is a psychologist with a full therapy caseload of clients dealing with depression, anxiety, eating disorders, family conflicts, parenting issues, and divorce. Many of her clients send her anxious texts, emails, and voicemails between sessions seeking her help in solving day-to-day problems and crises. Sometimes the lawyers for the divorce clients even contact her wanting to talk—immediately.

Step 1: Setting Limits

Dr. Wilson tells her clients that they should only contact her in an emergency. Most of them respect that. But some of them *feel* like they have an emergency situation when by Dr. Wilson's standards it is not an emergency. She is tired of explaining to them that their urgent issue is a problem to address during the counseling and to please not contact her for these types of issues. She is exhausted from responding to these communications all day in between her regular therapy sessions. She decides to get some consultation on what she can do.

Step 2: Imposing Consequences

After consultation, Dr. Wilson decides to hand out the following protocol to all new and old clients:

I am happy to work with you in our therapy sessions and look forward to assisting in your personal growth. I also understand that issues come up in between therapy sessions. Just to let you know, I am not set up to be an emergency service or crisis intervention service, so if you have a medical or psychological emergency, please call 911. If a problem arises that you want to discuss with me earlier than our scheduled next therapy session, you can briefly describe the problem in an email and I will decide if I believe we need to meet earlier. Just to let you know, I respond to shorter emails first. I respect your time and your concerns.

Dr. Wilson debated with herself whether to give out her cell phone number and decided against it going forward, even though she had done that in the past.

The problem she still struggled with was deciding which emails to respond to right away and which ones to tell the clients to save for the next therapy session. But with this new protocol she gained confidence and realized the she was actually helping her clients by demonstrating how they could set limits in their own relationships.

How Did Dr. Wilson Answer the Five Questions?

1. ***Is the consequence proportional to the limit I have set?***
   Yes. Not responding to every crisis call herself is proportional to the clients' need to learn more self-management skills. Plus, if it is really an emergency they should call 911.
2. ***Have I considered both positive and negative consequences?***
   Yes. The positive consequence of a shorter email message is that I will respond sooner. The negative consequence of a longer one is that I will respond later.
3. ***Is the consequence safe?***
   Yes. Having them call 911 is safe.
4. ***Am I ready to enforce my consequence?***
   Yes. I am exhausted.
5. ***Do I need to get help in imposing my consequence?***
   Yes. I got consultation on how to manage my caseload. It really helped.

Step 2½: EAR Statement (or Not)

This is a situation in which EAR Statements are very appropriate as therapy clients often have a lot of emotional needs and are looking for empathy, attention, and respect. In this case, Dr. Wilson said she understood that "issues come up between sessions," which shows some empathy and she said she respected their "time and concerns." Since her job is to pay attention during her therapy sessions, she has pretty much touched on all three possible factors of the EAR Statement. She will also be able to discuss her protocol during sessions with each client.

Discussion

This situation is a common problem for any professional who

deals with anxious clients. What they perceive as an emergency may or may not be what the professionals see. By having such a limit on between-session contacts, Dr. Wilson has more energy for her clients during their sessions. She had to get some consultation and build some assertiveness in order to do this. She worried that she would be perceived as in insensitive therapist. But the outcome was that her clients respected her more for clearly setting limits and taking care of herself.

THE DEMANDING LAW CLIENT

Background

Ms. Howe sought out Mr. Curtis to be her attorney in her divorce from a man she said was a very shady character.

Ms. HOWE: "I can't trust him for a minute. I'm sure he's going to try to take everything I own away from me."

Mr. CURTIS: "Actually, there are rules and procedures to ensure that you each get what is fair and proper. In fact, that is one of the first tasks that we need to do. That is to fill out this disclosure form of all of your Assets and Debts, including what you acquired together and what you acquired separately."

Ms. HOWE: "I'll put down what we acquired together. But I'm not going to put down the jewelry that my mother gave me before she died. It's worth over $50,000 and it's in a safe in Europe where my mother used to live. I'm not going to mention that. He has no right to it."

Mr. CURTIS: "Well, actually, you still need to list it on the form. If you got it as a gift or as an inheritance, then it will be assigned to you as your separate property. He has no right to it and no right to any value from it. That's the law in our state."

Ms. HOWE: "But I don't trust him for a minute. He will lie and claim that we got it together or that he gave it to me. I can't risk him to even know about it. Otherwise, he will do everything he can to take it from me, or at least half of its value."

Mr. CURIS: "The problem is that you need to put everything down on your Assets and Debts Disclosure Form so that he can at least ask questions about it. For example, he might claim that you bought the jewelry with money that you acquired together during the marriage and hid it away in Europe and that it really belongs to both of you 50-50. Then we produce any paperwork there is to prove that you were gifted it or inherited it. We also can challenge any paperwork that he says proves that you got it together. That's the standard procedure."

Ms. HOWE: "I'm not going to put it on the form."

Step 1: Setting Limits

Mr. CURTIS: "Well, you have to sign the form Under Penalty of Perjury that it's true and correct. And I can't submit paperwork that I know is false. I could lose my license to practice law."

Ms. HOWE: "I'm not going to put it on the form."

It became clear to Mr. CURTIS that simply setting the limit with her was not going to work. He would have to come up with a consequence to impose.

Step 2: Imposing Consequences

Mr. CURTIS: "You know what. It's the beginning of your case and no hearings are scheduled yet. So I'm going to give you a choice.

"Choice A: If you want to work with me, you will have to include the jewelry in Europe as your separate property on the Assets and Debts Disclosure Form.

"Choice B: If you don't put the jewelry on the form, then you will need to find another lawyer. I can't ethically represent you. I can understand that might be frustrating, but that's the rules."

Ms. HOWE: "That's an easy choice. Then I won't be working with you. And I would like my retainer back."

Mr. CURTIS: "That's fine. I will write you a check right now. Here you go. Best wishes."

Ms. HOWE: "Too bad. But that's my choice."

Mr. CURTIS: "That's okay. I respect your decision. Best wishes."

How Did Mr. Curtis Answer the Five Questions?

1. ***Is the consequence proportional to the limit I have set?***
   Yes. She wants me to lie and I can't do that. It's a direct and proportional consequence.
2. ***Have I considered both positive and negative consequences?***
   Yes. I actually gave her a choice. The positive consequence of disclosing her jewelry and the negative choice of not working with me. But she sees that as a positive.
3. ***Is the consequence safe?***
   Yes. That's not an issue here.
4. ***Am I ready to enforce my consequence?***
   Yes. I won't take her case and will give her a full refund.
5. ***Do I need to get help in imposing my consequence?***
   No. It's easy not to take her case and not to do work on her case.

Step 2½: EAR Statement (or Not)

Mr. Curtis decided to give her two simple EAR Statements? "I can understand that might be frustrating...." (Empathy) and "I respect your decision." (Respect) It was not essential to give an EAR Statement as they were ending their business relationship. However, EAR can calm the ending and avoid having an angry client leaving the office and telling the world how terrible the lawyer is. For people in any profession, the biggest thing you have going for you is your reputation, so it's good to use EAR to keep clients calm, so they don't feel tempted to harm it.

Discussion

This situation could arise with any professional relationship anywhere. Professions have ethical standards that must be followed or the professional may face consequences—including losing a license to practice their profession. High-conflict clients, in particular, want professionals to bend the rules in their favor. The need for setting limits is common in this area. It also may require imposing consequences to stop the client's inappropriate behavior.

In this case, the lawyer gave the client a choice. That option isn't always available, but it worked well here. High-conflict people react negatively to being directly told what to do, especially when they feel criticized. By giving the client a choice, it can defuse most of the feeling of being trapped. In this case, the client felt good about her choice and didn't seem angry at her lawyer. They were able to part on good terms.

One other point about ending relationships with potentially high-conflict clients: While Mr. Curtis could have deducted from the retainer the hour or two that he had worked on this case, he may have saved more in the long run by giving the whole retainer back. An hour or two isn't too much lost income and it may be worth a lot more in good will with the client, especially if she is potentially a high-conflict client.

Conclusion

Professionals often handle problems that their clients or someone else in their lives have created. The professional-client relationship has lots of opportunities for conflict to arise. Telling the client from the start how the professional works with their clients can be very helpful so that there are no surprises. Setting limits is best done when it can be done in advance. But it is also clear that there will be times with high-conflict clients when consequences need to be threatened or imposed. These examples demonstrated some easy ways to set limits in advance and how providing choices is a good alternative to clients feeling trapped.

CHAPTER 15

IT'S UP TO YOU

This book has presented a very simple method for setting limits and imposing consequences in 2½ steps. However, while it looks easy it can be hard depending on the situation and your level of confidence in Setting the Limits and Imposing your Consequences (SLIC Solutions). When potentially high-conflict people are involved it can be especially challenging. That is why we want to end this book with some encouraging words that you can remind yourself.

Worldwide in the 21st century, it is important for all of us to learn how to set limits AND impose consequences when necessary. The more people who learn this SLIC skill, the easier it will be for you and everyone else. Every individual is an important part of this learning and building process. You are an important part of helping the world become more peaceful and responsible.

Most people do not like to set limits on other adults' behavior and almost everyone has an especially hard time *imposing consequences* on other adults who are acting badly. At the start of the book, we emphasized preparing to assert yourself. We encourage you to get support from friends and family in gaining the confidence and experience necessary to use SLIC solutions. Almost everyone has difficulty with this, so you are not alone. You can help them too.

High-conflict people (HCPs) seem to be about ten percent of the adult population now around the world. In many cases, they were born this way or became this way from painful early childhood experiences. They see all relationships as inherently adversarial, as win-lose, so it takes more effort on our part to try to turn our interactions with them into win-win situations. We don't do them or us a favor if we tolerate high-conflict behavior from them that hurts us and those we care about. By clearly setting limits, we give them a chance to adjust their behavior to be more cooperative and civil. By firmly imposing consequences to help them learn and to stop them from engaging in harmful behaviors does them a favor as well as us. (Remember the young Gilbert Goons who ended up in prison because the adults tolerated their behavior and didn't impose consequences at an earlier age.) Imposing consequences is a positive and necessary skill.

To be most comfortable and effective, we encourage you to practice, practice, practice using this skill. Find a friend or family member who you can role-play with before going into a SLIC situation. As explained early in this book, practice two different ways:

First, play the part of the person you want to set limits on and have your role-play partner pretend to be you. Then say to your partner what you expect that person might say to you. Try to think of all of their challenging comments to your efforts to set limits.

Second, switch roles and play yourself and have your role-play partner be the person you are setting limits on. This way you will be prepared and more confident in responding to every challenge that you get. (Remember how prepared the hospital administrator was when she was setting limits and threatening to impose a consequence on the doctor.)

We also emphasized the use of EAR Statements throughout this book. This is a very important tool, especially when there is an ongoing relationship. The goal is positive future behavior change, rather than punishment. It's easy to get this backwards and EAR Statements will help you explain the positive benefits of using new, more desirable behavior. EAR Statements will help you feel better about imposing consequences as well.

On the other hand, it is important to avoid being "too nice" when you are dealing with people who are manipulative by nature and will twist any statement of empathy or respect in order to undermine your efforts to set necessary limits or impose necessary consequences. Stay firm and focused on your desired outcome rather than succumbing to their efforts to talk you out of your SLIC solution. In about half of situations, giving an EAR Statement is not recommended. Feel free to discuss with a role-play partner whether to give an EAR Statement or not in any particular situation.

Throughout this book we have tried to provide a wide cross section of potential conflicts in today's world. While your type of conflict may not have been included here, the book has such a wide range of examples that one or two may be similar to what you are looking for. A lot of the limits and consequences can be applied in many different settings. It is the fundamental process of setting the limit, imposing the consequence, and giving an EAR Statement (or not) that seems to fit almost every situation.

In short, you have learned the tools. You have seen them in action. You know that SLIC works in real-life situations: at work, at home, in your community, and even with those who seem impossible to deal with.

You cannot change every high-conflict person. You cannot make them suddenly become "nice" or magically become empathetic. However, you can protect yourself. You can take control of your boundaries, preserve your energy, and reduce conflict before it escalates. That is true power.

SLIC is more than just a method; it's a path to freedom, clarity, and confidence. Embrace it. Practice it. Own it. Your life is worth it. Use your voice. Set your limits. Impose your consequences. Walk away when you need to. Show empathy when it works. But always remember: your peace, your energy, your well-being—these are yours to protect. You can do this!

Appendix A

List of SLIC Sample Situations and Responses

Appendix B

SLIC Journal Worksheet

Setting Your Limits and Imposing Your Consequences

Name / Date: ______________________________

Location / Context: ______________________________

1. Describe the Situation

- Who was involved?
- What happened? (Brief summary)

____

____

____

2. Difficult Behavior Observed

- Aggression (verbal, physical, online)
- Manipulation / Gaslighting
- Boundary violations
- Disrespect / dismissive behavior
- Other: ______________________________
- Notes / Examples:

____

____

____

3. Limits Set

- What limits did you communicate? (Be specific)

- Method: [ ] Verbal [ ] Written [ ] Digital / Other
- Notes:

____

____

____

4. **Consequences Imposed**

- What consequences were applied? (e.g., blocking, reporting, refusing request, legal action)
- Immediate outcome:

____

____

____

5. **EAR Statements** (if used)

- Empathy: ______________________________
- Attention: ______________________________
- Respect: ______________________________

6. **Outcome & Reflection**

- How did the other person respond?
- Did the limit/consequence work?
- What worked well? _________________________
- What could be improved next time?

____

____

____

7. **Patterns & Triggers**

- Any recurring behaviors or triggers you noticed?
- Insights for future interactions:

____

____

8. **Next Steps / Follow-Up**

- Actions to take (legal, professional, personal):

____

____

- Reminders for follow-up:

____

____

Tip: Fill out the journal as soon as possible after each interaction. Over time, patterns will emerge, helping you recognize high-conflict behaviors earlier and refine your responses.

References

Bill Eddy, *High Conflict People in Legal Disputes, 2nd Ed.* 2016.

Bill Eddy, *Our New World of Adult Bullies*. 2024.

Lisa McCubbin, *Betty Ford: First Lady, Women's Advocate, Survivor, Trailblazer.* 2018.

Rachel Monroe, "Growing Pains," *The New Yorker*, July 1, 2024.

Epic Games, Inc. v. Google LLC (In re Google Play Store Antitrust Litig.), Nos. 24-6256, 24-6274 25-303, 2025 U.S. App. LEXIS 19185 (9th Cir. July 31, 2025)

Acknowledgements

To my law school professor, Bill Eddy, whose wisdom, mentorship, and collaboration helped bring this book to life.

—Ekaterina Ricci

I want to acknowledge my wife, Alice, who consistently provides wisdom and feedback for my books. (And thanks, Alice, for setting limits on me to reach a good work-life balance while writing this book and taking time off for travel!) I appreciate Ekaterina Ricci for suggesting that we write this book and for being such a flexible and prolific co-author. I thank our team at High Conflict Institute, especially Megan Hunter, CEO, for your going leadership and encouraging this project, and to Susie Rayner, Meggen Romine, and Liz Hunter for providing ongoing support over the past few years which enabled me to focus on writing in between presentations and consultations. I also want to acknowledge a few clients who shared their stories with me and inspired some of the confidential situations described in this book. You know who you are.

—Bill Eddy

The Authors

Bill Eddy, LCSW, Esq. is a globally recognized thought leader on high-conflict behavior and the co-founder and Director of Innovation of the High Conflict Institute. A pioneer in the development of High Conflict Personality Theory (HCP), he has transformed the fields of law, mental health, and dispute resolution with practical frameworks for managing individuals with high-conflict traits. Bill has over four decades of professional experience as a family law attorney, Licensed Clinical Social Worker, and senior mediator, including 15 years as Senior Family Mediator at the National Conflict Resolution Center. He has served on the faculty of the renowned Straus Institute for Dispute Resolution at Pepperdine University School of Law and held an academic appointment at the University of Newcastle Law School in Australia. An internationally sought-after keynote speaker and trainer, Bill has presented in over 40 U.S. states and 14 countries. He is the author of more than twenty books and writes a widely read blog on Psychology Today with over six million views.

HighConflictInstitute.com / ConflictInfluencer.com

Ekaterina Ricci, MDR, MLS, is a dispute resolution expert and legal consultant specializing in cross-border negotiations, international diplomacy, and high-conflict dynamics. She is recognized for her interdisciplinary approach to resolving complex disputes where legal systems, organizational power structures, and cultural identities intersect. Ekaterina has served as a mediator, consultant, and policy advisor in international commercial and institutional disputes, contributing to resolution efforts in legal and multilateral settings. Her work draws on over a decade of experience integrating behavioral science, legal analysis, and narrative strategy to address high-stakes conflicts in courts, international forums, and corporate environments. She holds dual master's degrees in Dispute Resolution and Legal Studies from Pepperdine Caruso School of Law, and a B.S. in Microbiology, Immunology, and Molecular Genetics from UCLA. She completed advanced training in diplomacy and international law through UN programs in Geneva. Ekaterina also teaches and speaks on conflict systems, trauma-informed mediation, and cross-cultural negotiation.

www.ingramcontent.com/pod-product-compliance
Lightning Source LLC
Jackson TN
JSHW071211141125
94118JS00002B/2

* 9 7 8 1 9 5 0 0 5 7 4 7 4 *